SEBASTIAN CROITORIU

The Business Owner's Guide to Digital Marketing Success

Copyright © 2024 by Sebastian Croitoriu

All rights reserved. No part of this publication may be reproduced, stored or transmitted in any form or by any means, electronic, mechanical, photocopying, recording, scanning, or otherwise without written permission from the publisher. It is illegal to copy this book, post it to a website, or distribute it by any other means without permission.

First edition

This book was professionally typeset on Reedsy. Find out more at reedsy.com

Contents

1	Summary	1
2	Introduction	4
3	Building Your Online Foundation	7
4	Attracting Your Ideal Customers	22
5	Creating Content That Converts	53
6	Paid Advertising Demystified: Your Fast Track to Growth	63
7	Refine and Conquer: Your Data-Driven Playbook for Digital…	83
8	Investing in Your Digital Future: A Smart Budgeting Guide…	90
9	Building a Strong Brand Presence: Crafting a Story That…	100
10	Local SEO: Dominating Your Local Market	109
11	Future-Proof Your Marketing: Embracing Innovation for…	116
12	Your Digital Marketing Toolkit: Resources for Success	123
13	Your Journey to Digital Marketing Mastery	129

1

Summary

"The Business Owner's Guide to Digital Marketing Success" is a practical, actionable, and comprehensive guide for entrepreneurs and small business owners who want to harness the power of digital marketing to grow their businesses. Written by Sebastian Croitoriu, a seasoned digital marketing expert with years of experience helping businesses succeed online, this book cuts through the noise and delivers a clear roadmap for navigating the digital landscape.

The book begins by emphasizing the importance of building a strong online foundation, starting with a well-designed, high-converting website and a compelling brand identity. It then delves into various digital marketing channels, including search engine optimization (SEO), social media marketing, email marketing, content marketing, and paid advertising. Each chapter provides a clear explanation of the strategies and tactics involved, along with actionable tips, quick wins, and real-world case studies to illustrate their effectiveness.

Throughout the book, Sebastian Croitoriu shares his expertise and insights, guiding readers through the process of setting realistic goals, crafting effective campaigns, tracking results, and optimizing their strategies for maximum ROI. He emphasizes the importance of data-driven decision-making and provides practical tools and resources that business owners can use to implement these strategies effectively.

The book also covers emerging trends in digital marketing, such as artificial intelligence (AI), voice search, and video marketing, offering guidance on how businesses can leverage these technologies to stay ahead of the curve. It concludes with a call to action, encouraging readers to take the knowledge they've gained and apply it to their businesses to achieve lasting growth in the digital age.

Key Takeaways:

Digital marketing is essential for business growth in today's world.

Small businesses can achieve significant results with a well-planned and executed digital marketing strategy.

Understanding your target audience and creating buyer personas is crucial for effective marketing.

A strong online foundation, starting with a well-designed website and a compelling brand identity, is essential for success.

SEO, social media marketing, email marketing, content marketing, and paid advertising are all valuable tools for attracting and engaging customers.

Tracking your results and making data-driven decisions is key to optimizing your marketing efforts.

Staying up-to-date with emerging trends and technologies can help you stay ahead of the competition.

"The Business Owner's Guide to Digital Marketing Success"

SUMMARY

is a must-read for any entrepreneur or small business owner who wants to unlock the full potential of digital marketing and achieve sustainable growth in the digital age.

2

Introduction

Are you a business owner feeling overwhelmed by the ever-changing world of digital marketing? Do you find yourself spending countless hours researching strategies, only to be bombarded with complex jargon and conflicting advice? Do you wish there was a simple, straightforward guide that could help you navigate this digital landscape and actually see results?

If so, then you've come to the right place.

My name is Sebastian Croitoriu, and I've spent the past ten years immersed in the world of digital marketing. I started my journey by building my own successful clothing brand, where I learned firsthand the power of digital marketing to drive sales and grow a business. I then transitioned into helping other businesses achieve their goals, eventually opening my own marketing agency.

Throughout my career as a media buyer, I've worked with a diverse range of companies, from startups to established brands, across various industries. I've seen firsthand the challenges that business owners face when it comes to digital marketing—the

INTRODUCTION

lack of time, the confusion around different strategies, and the difficulty of measuring results.

That's why I've written "The Business Owner's Guide to Digital Marketing Success"—your no-nonsense playbook for harnessing the power of the internet to grow your business. I understand that as a busy entrepreneur, your time is precious, and you need a solution that's both effective and efficient.

That's why I've created this book: to cut through the noise and deliver a clear, actionable roadmap for achieving digital marketing success. No fluff, no filler—just the essential strategies and tactics that will help you attract new customers, boost your brand visibility, and drive real growth for your business.

What Sets This Book Apart

Unlike other digital marketing guides that are either too broad or too technical, this book focuses on the specific needs and challenges of small to medium-sized business owners. We'll share real-world examples of businesses just like yours that have successfully implemented digital marketing strategies on a limited budget. We'll provide step-by-step instructions, templates, and checklists that you can use to take action immediately.

Most importantly, we'll teach you how to measure your results and track your return on investment (ROI). Because at the end of the day, what matters most is not just generating traffic or getting likes on social media—it's about driving real business growth.

Your Journey to Digital Marketing Success Starts Now

Whether you're a complete novice or have dabbled in digital marketing before, this book will equip you with the knowledge and tools you need to take your business to the next level. By the end, you'll have a solid understanding of the core principles of digital marketing, a clear action plan for implementing effective campaigns, and the confidence to navigate the ever-evolving digital landscape.

So, are you ready to unlock the full potential of digital marketing for your business? Let's dive in!

3

Building Your Online Foundation

In the digital age, your website is your virtual storefront, your 24/7 salesperson, and your most powerful tool for connecting with potential customers. A well-crafted website not only establishes your brand's credibility but also serves as a hub for generating leads, driving sales, and fostering customer loyalty.

Whether you're a seasoned entrepreneur or just starting out, your website is the cornerstone of your online presence. Let's explore the essential elements of creating a high-converting website and crafting a compelling brand identity that will set you apart from the competition.

Creating a High-Converting Website

Think of your website as your digital storefront. It's the first impression many potential customers will have of your business. A well-designed, user-friendly website can make the difference between a casual visitor and a loyal customer.

Why Your Website is Your Digital Storefront

A well-designed website:

- **Establishes Credibility:** A professional website signals that you are a legitimate business and that you take your brand seriously.
- **Attracts New Customers:** A user-friendly website with valuable content can attract potential customers through search engines and social media.
- **Generates Leads and Sales:** By including clear calls to action (CTAs) and lead capture forms, your website can convert visitors into paying customers.
- **Builds Customer Relationships:** A website with engaging content and a strong brand personality can foster loyalty and repeat business.

Website Planning Worksheet

Before diving into the design and development of your website, it's crucial to have a clear plan in place. Use this worksheet to define your website's goals, target audience, key messages, content strategy, and calls to action:

1. **What are the main goals of your website?** (e.g., generate leads, sell products, provide information, build brand awareness)
2. **Who is your target audience?** (e.g., demographics, interests, pain points)
3. **What are the key messages you want to convey?** (e.g., what makes your business unique, what problems you solve, what value you offer)
4. **What kind of content will you create?** (e.g., blog posts, product descriptions, videos, testimonials)
5. **What calls to action will you use?** (e.g., "Shop Now," "Learn More," "Contact Us")

By answering these questions, you'll have a solid foundation for creating a website that is both effective and aligned with your business goals.

Essential Elements of a User-Friendly Website

Creating a high-converting website doesn't have to be complicated. Here are the essential elements to focus on:

- **Clean and Intuitive Design:** Your website should be visually appealing and easy to navigate. Avoid clutter and use a simple, uncluttered layout with plenty of white space. A clear visual hierarchy, achieved through the use of headings, subheadings, and bullet points, helps guide visitors through your content. Choose a color scheme that aligns with your brand and creates a pleasant user experience, avoiding harsh contrasts or overly bright colors. Use easy-to-read fonts like Arial, Helvetica, or Open Sans, and consider incorporating high-quality images or videos to break up text and enhance visual appeal.

- **Clear Calls to Action:** Tell your visitors what you want them to do (e.g., "Shop Now," "Learn More," "Contact Us"). Make these CTAs prominent and easy to find by using contrasting colors, larger font sizes, or eye-catching buttons. Place CTAs strategically throughout your website, such as at the end of blog posts, on your homepage, and in sidebars. Use action-oriented language that encourages clicks (e.g., "Get Started," "Discover More").

- **Mobile Responsiveness:** More people are browsing the internet on their smartphones than ever before. Ensure your website adapts seamlessly to different screen sizes by using a responsive design. This means that your website will automatically adjust its layout and content to fit the screen it's being viewed on, whether it's a desktop computer, tablet, or smartphone. Test your website on various devices to ensure a smooth experience for all users.

- **Fast Loading Speed:** People are impatient, and slow-loading websites can lead to high bounce rates (visitors leaving your site quickly). Optimize your images by compressing them without sacrificing quality. Minify your code to reduce file sizes. Use a reliable web hosting provider that can deliver fast loading speeds. Consider using a content delivery network (CDN) to distribute your website's content across multiple servers, improving load times for users in different locations.

- **Compelling Content:** Your website content should be informative, engaging, and relevant to your target audience. Use clear, concise language, and break up text with visuals like images, infographics, or videos. Focus on providing value to your readers by addressing their pain points and offering solutions. Use a conversational tone to make your content more approachable and relatable. Incorporate keywords that your target audience is likely to search for, but avoid keyword stuffing, which can harm your search engine rankings.

- **Contact Information:** Make it easy for visitors to contact you by prominently displaying your phone number, email address, and social media links in the header or footer of your website. Consider adding a contact form for visitors to send you messages directly. If you have a physical location, include your address and a map for easy directions.

·

Real-World Example:
Mom's Homemade Pies, a small bakery, launched a website with a simple, rustic design featuring mouthwatering images of their pies. They included an easy-to-use online ordering system and prominently displayed their contact information and location. Within weeks, their online orders increased by 30%, demonstrating the power of a well-designed website.

Learning from the Worst: Examples of Bad Website Design
To further illustrate the importance of a well-designed website, let's take a look at a few examples of what *not* to do:

- **Cluttered Layout:** A website crammed with too much text, images, and flashy elements can overwhelm visitors and make it difficult to find the information they need.
- **Confusing Navigation:** A website with a convoluted menu structure or unclear labels can frustrate visitors and make it difficult for them to find what they're looking for.
- **Slow Loading Speed:** A website that takes forever to load will drive visitors away before they even have a chance to see your content.
- **Lack of Mobile Responsiveness:** A website that doesn't adapt to different screen sizes will look distorted and be difficult to use on mobile devices, leading to a poor user experience.

By avoiding these common pitfalls, you can ensure that your website is user-friendly and effective at achieving your business

goals.
Website Design on a Budget
You don't need a massive budget to create a professional-looking website. Here are a few tips:

- **Website Builders:** Consider using platforms like Wix, Squarespace, or WordPress. These user-friendly tools offer customizable templates and drag-and-drop functionality, making it easy to create a website even if you have no coding experience. They also offer affordable monthly plans that include hosting and domain registration.
- **Affordable Templates:** Many website builders and marketplaces like ThemeForest or Creative Market offer affordable, professionally designed templates that you can customize to match your brand. These templates often include pre-designed pages, color schemes, and fonts, saving you time and effort.
- **Stock Photos:** Use high-quality stock photos from websites like Unsplash or Pexels to enhance the visual appeal of your website. These websites offer a vast selection of free or affordable images that you can use to create a professional look without hiring a photographer.

Website Content That Converts
Your website content plays a crucial role in converting visitors into customers. Here's what to focus on:

- **Know Your Audience:** Tailor your content to the specific needs and interests of your target audience. What problems are they trying to solve? What information are they looking for? What are their pain points? Conduct market research

and create buyer personas to better understand your ideal customers. This will help you create content that resonates with them and addresses their specific needs.
- **Provide Value:** Offer valuable information that educates, entertains, or solves a problem for your audience. This could include blog posts, articles, how-to guides, videos, or downloadable resources like e-books or checklists. By providing valuable content, you position yourself as an expert in your field and build trust with your audience.
- **Use a Clear Call to Action:** Tell your visitors what you want them to do after reading your content. Do you want them to sign up for your email list, purchase a product, or contact you for more information? Make this clear by using strong verbs and concise language. Ensure your CTAs are visually prominent and easy to click. Use different types of CTAs throughout your website, such as buttons, text links, and pop-ups, to cater to different user preferences.

Measuring Website Success: Using Data to Drive Decisions

You've put in the effort to create a beautiful and functional website. Now, it's time to understand how visitors are interacting with it. This is where website analytics comes into play. By tracking key metrics, you can gain valuable insights into your audience, their behavior, and the effectiveness of your website.

Key Metrics to Track:

- **Website Traffic:** This refers to the number of visitors who come to your website. You can track overall traffic, traffic from specific sources (e.g., search engines, social

media, referrals), and the most popular pages on your site. Understanding where your traffic is coming from helps you identify which marketing channels are working and which need improvement.
- **Bounce Rate:** This is the percentage of visitors who leave your website after viewing only one page. A high bounce rate could indicate that your content isn't relevant or engaging, or that your website is difficult to navigate. Analyzing bounce rates can help you pinpoint areas for improvement in your website's content, design, or user experience.
- **Time on Page:** This measures how long visitors stay on each page of your website. Longer time on page usually indicates that visitors are finding your content valuable and engaging. Tracking this metric helps you understand which pages are resonating with your audience and where you might need to improve content or calls to action.
- **Conversion Rate:** This is the percentage of visitors who take a desired action on your website, such as making a purchase, filling out a contact form, or signing up for your email list. Monitoring your conversion rate is crucial for understanding how effective your website is at turning visitors into customers or leads.

Using Google Analytics (or Other Tools):

Google Analytics is a powerful free tool that provides detailed insights into your website traffic and user behavior. It allows you to track the metrics mentioned above, as well as many others, such as user demographics, interests, and devices used. By setting up goals and tracking conversions, you can see which pages and strategies are most effective at driving desired actions.

Other website analytics tools you might consider include:

- **Matomo (formerly Piwik):** An open-source alternative to Google Analytics, Matomo offers similar features with greater privacy controls.
- **Clicky:** Provides real-time analytics and heatmaps, showing you where visitors are clicking on your website.
- **Hotjar:** Offers recordings of user sessions, allowing you to see how visitors interact with your website, as well as heatmaps and surveys.

How to Use Website Analytics Data:

By analyzing your website analytics data, you can identify trends, patterns, and opportunities for improvement. For example:

- If you notice that a particular blog post is attracting a lot of traffic but has a high bounce rate, you might consider revising the content to make it more engaging or relevant.
- If you see that visitors are leaving your site from a particular page, you might try to optimize that page's content, design, or calls to action.
- If your conversion rate is low, you might experiment with different CTAs, landing page designs, or product offerings.

Remember, website analytics is not just about collecting data. It's about using that data to make informed decisions that will improve your website's performance and help you achieve your business goals.

Quick Wins for Website Optimization:

Here are a few quick tips for using website analytics to improve your website:

- **Identify Your Top-Performing Pages:** Focus on promoting and optimizing your most popular pages to drive even more traffic and conversions.
- **Fix High Bounce Rate Pages:** Analyze pages with high bounce rates to understand why visitors are leaving and make necessary improvements.
- **Optimize Your Conversion Funnel:** Track your visitors' journey through your website and identify any bottlenecks or areas where they are dropping off. Make adjustments to improve the flow and encourage visitors to take the desired actions.
- **Experiment with Different Strategies:** Test different versions of your website, landing pages, or CTAs to see what works best for your audience. A/B testing can be a valuable tool for identifying the most effective elements of your website.

Website Security: Protecting Your Online Assets

In today's digital landscape, website security is more important than ever. Hackers and cybercriminals are constantly looking for vulnerabilities to exploit, and your website is a potential target. A security breach can result in data loss, financial damage, and reputational harm.

Key Security Measures:

- **Secure Sockets Layer (SSL) Certificate:** An SSL certificate encrypts data transmitted between your website and visitors' browsers, protecting sensitive information like credit

card numbers and personal data. It also displays a padlock icon in the browser's address bar, indicating to visitors that your website is secure.
- **Strong Passwords:** Use strong, unique passwords for your website's admin panel and other login areas. Avoid using easily guessable passwords like "password123" or your birthdate. Consider using a password manager to help you generate and store complex passwords.
- **Regular Backups:** Regularly back up your website's data so you can restore it in case of a security breach or other disaster. You can use a plugin or service that automatically backs up your website to the cloud.
- **Web Application Firewall (WAF):** A WAF acts as a barrier between your website and potential attacks, filtering out malicious traffic and blocking known vulnerabilities. Many web hosting providers offer WAF services as part of their packages.
- **Security Plugins and Updates:** If you're using a content management system like WordPress, install security plugins like Wordfence or iThemes Security. Keep your CMS, plugins, and themes updated to patch any vulnerabilities that hackers could exploit.

Quick Wins for Website Security:

- **Update Your Software:** Keep your website's software, including your CMS, plugins, and themes, up to date. Software updates often include security patches that fix vulnerabilities.
- **Use Strong Passwords:** Avoid using simple or common passwords, and never reuse passwords across different

websites. Use a combination of upper and lowercase letters, numbers, and symbols.
- **Be Wary of Phishing Emails:** Be cautious of emails that ask for your login credentials or other sensitive information. Legitimate companies rarely ask for this information via email.
- **Educate Your Employees:** If you have employees who have access to your website, train them on basic security practices, such as using strong passwords and being wary of phishing emails.
- **Regularly Scan for Malware:** Use a website security scanner to check your website for malware and other vulnerabilities.

Accessibility: Making Your Website Inclusive for Everyone

Website accessibility refers to the practice of designing and developing websites that can be used by people with disabilities. This includes people with visual, auditory, motor, and cognitive impairments. Making your website accessible is not only the right thing to do but also a legal requirement in many countries. It also expands your potential audience and can improve your website's search engine rankings.

Accessibility Checklist:

Use this checklist to evaluate your website's accessibility:

- **Alt Text for Images:** Provide alternative text descriptions for all images on your website. This allows screen readers to describe images to users who are visually impaired.
- **Sufficient Color Contrast:** Ensure that there is enough contrast between the text and background colors on your website so that people with visual impairments can easily

read the content.
- **Keyboard Navigation:** Make sure all elements of your website can be accessed and interacted with using a keyboard alone. This is important for people who cannot use a mouse.
- **Clear and Concise Language:** Use simple language and avoid jargon or technical terms that may be difficult for some users to understand.
- **Captions and Transcripts for Videos:** Provide captions and transcripts for videos on your website so that people who are deaf or hard of hearing can access the content.
- **Proper Heading Structure:** Use headings and subheadings to organize your content and make it easier for screen readers to navigate.

Quick Wins for Accessibility:

- **Use a Website Accessibility Checker:** There are many free and paid tools available that can help you evaluate your website's accessibility and identify areas for improvement.
- **Choose Accessible Themes and Plugins:** If you're using a CMS like WordPress, choose themes and plugins that are designed with accessibility in mind.
- **Get Feedback from Users with Disabilities:** Ask people with disabilities to test your website andprovide feedback on its accessibility.

Quick Wins for Website Optimization and Brand Building

Here are a few additional quick wins to help you optimize your website and strengthen your brand:

- **Optimize Your Website for Local Search:** If your business serves a specific geographic area, optimize your website for local search by including your location in your website content and metadata. Claim your Google My Business listing and ensure it is accurate and up-to-date.
- **Create a Google My Business Listing:** A Google My Business listing allows your business to appear in Google Maps and local search results. It's a free and easy way to improve your visibility in local search and provide potential customers with essential information about your business, such as your address, phone number, and hours of operation.
- **Use Social Media to Showcase Your Brand Personality:** Social media platforms are a great way to showcase your brand's personality and connect with your audience on a more personal level. Share engaging content, interact with your followers, and use a consistent voice and tone that aligns with your brand identity.

A Brief Discussion of Website Platforms

Choosing the right website platform is crucial for building a successful online presence. Here's a brief overview of the most popular options:

- **Website Builders:** Platforms like Wix, Squarespace, and Weebly are ideal for beginners and small businesses with limited technical expertise. They offer easy-to-use drag-and-drop interfaces, customizable templates, and affordable pricing plans.
- **WordPress:** WordPress is a powerful and flexible content management system (CMS) that powers over 40% of web-

sites on the internet. It offers a wide range of themes and plugins, allowing you to create any type of website you can imagine. However, it requires a bit more technical knowledge than website builders.
- **Shopify:** Shopify is a leading e-commerce platform designed specifically for online stores. It offers a range of features for managing products, inventory, payments, and shipping. If you're planning to sell products online, Shopify is a great option.
- **Custom-Built Websites:** For large businesses or those with very specific needs, a custom-built website may be the best option. However, custom websites can be expensive and require ongoing maintenance.

The best platform for your business will depend on your budget, technical skills, and specific needs. Consider factors like ease of use, flexibility, scalability, and cost when making your decision.

4

Attracting Your Ideal Customers

With a solid online foundation in place, it's time to focus on attracting your ideal customers. This chapter will explore the most effective digital marketing channels and strategies for reaching your target audience, building relationships, and driving traffic to your website.

Understanding Your Target Audience

Before diving into specific marketing tactics, it's crucial to have a deep understanding of your target audience. This means knowing their demographics (age, gender, location), interests, pain points, and online behavior. By creating detailed buyer personas, you can tailor your marketing messages and campaigns to resonate with your ideal customers.

What are Buyer Personas?

Buyer personas are fictional representations of your ideal customers. They help you understand your target audience on a deeper level, beyond just basic demographics. By creating buyer personas, you can identify your customers' motivations, goals, and challenges. This allows you to create marketing messages and campaigns that speak directly to their needs and interests.

How to Create Buyer Personas:

1. **Conduct Market Research:** Gather data about your existing customers through surveys, interviews, and feedback.
2. **Analyze Your Competitors:** Research your competitors' target audience and identify any gaps or opportunities in the market.
3. **Identify Demographics:** Define the age, gender, location, income level, education level, and other relevant demographic information of your ideal customers.
4. **Identify Psychographics:** Determine your customers' interests, values, lifestyles, and online behavior.
5. **Identify Pain Points:** What problems are your customers facing? What challenges are they trying to overcome?
6. **Identify Goals:** What are your customers' goals and aspirations? How can your products or services help them achieve those goals?

Example Buyer Persona:

- **Name:** Sarah
- **Age:** 35
- **Occupation:** Marketing Manager
- **Location:** New York City
- **Pain Points:** Sarah is struggling to manage her company's social media presence and generate leads.
- **Goals:** Sarah wants to increase brand awareness, attract new customers, and drive sales through social media.

By understanding Sarah's pain points and goals, you can create content and campaigns that speak directly to her needs, such as a blog post on social media strategies for lead generation or a free webinar on social media advertising.

Quick Tip:

Create multiple buyer personas to represent different segments of your target audience. This will help you tailor your marketing messages and campaigns more effectively.

Search Engine Optimization (SEO): Get Found Online

Search Engine Optimization (SEO) is the process of optimizing your website and content to rank higher in search engine results pages (SERPs). When potential customers search for keywords related to your business, you want your website to appear at the top of the search results. This can significantly increase your website traffic and attract qualified leads.

In the world of digital marketing, SEO is your silent salesperson, working tirelessly in the background to bring potential customers to your doorstep. It's like having a prime location on a bustling street, where everyone can easily find you.

SEO Fundamentals: The Building Blocks of Visibility

- **Keyword Research:** Before you start creating content or optimizing your website, it's crucial to identify the keywords and phrases your target audience is searching for. These are the words and phrases people type into search engines when looking for products or services like yours. Tools like Google Keyword Planner, SEMrush, or Ahrefs can help you find relevant keywords with high search volume and low competition. By strategically incorporating these keywords into your website content, you increase the chances of your website appearing in relevant search results.

- **On-Page Optimization:** Once you've identified your target keywords, it's time to optimize your website's content. This includes optimizing your title tags, meta descriptions, header tags (H1, H2, etc.), and image alt text with relevant keywords. Think of these elements as signposts that tell search engines what your page is about.

- **Content Creation:** Search engines love fresh, high-quality content. Regularly publish blog posts, articles, or other types of content that provide value to your audience and answer their questions. Use your target keywords naturally throughout your content, but avoid keyword stuffing, which can harm your search engine rankings.

- **Technical SEO:** Technical SEO involves optimizing the technical aspects of your website to make it easier for search engines to crawl and index your content. This includes ensuring your website has a clean code structure, fast loading speed, mobile responsiveness, and a secure connection (HTTPS). You can use tools like Google Search Console to identify and fix technical issues on your website.

- **Link Building:** Backlinks are links from other websites to yours. They act as votes of confidence, signaling to search engines that your website is trustworthy and authoritative. The more high-quality backlinks you have, the higher your website is likely to rank in search results. You can earn backlinks by creating shareable content, guest blogging on other websites, and reaching out to influencers or industry partners.

Quick Wins for SEO: Boost Your Rankings Fast

Here are a few quick and easy SEO tactics that can help you see immediate results:

- **Claim and Optimize Your Google My Business Listing:** If your business serves a local area, claiming and optimizing your Google My Business listing is essential for local SEO. Ensure your business information is accurate and up-to-date, add photos and videos, and encourage customers to leave reviews.
- **Optimize Your Website for Mobile:** With more than half of all web traffic coming from mobile devices, it's crucial to have a mobile-friendly website. Google prioritizes mobile-friendly websites in its search results, so if your website isn't optimized for mobile, you could be missing out on a significant amount of traffic.
- **Create a Sitemap:** A sitemap is a file that lists all the pages on your website. Submitting a sitemap to search engines helps them crawl and index your website more efficiently, potentially leading to faster and better indexing of your content.
- **Fix Broken Links:** Broken links can harm your SEO and frustrate users. Use a tool like Broken Link Checker to regularly scan your website for broken links and fix them promptly.

SEO Case Study: Pain Plaisir Bakery - A Taste of SEO Success

Pain Plaisir, a charming artisanal bakery nestled in the heart of Bucharest, was known for its delectable pastries, handcrafted bread, and warm, inviting atmosphere. However, despite rave reviews from loyal customers, they were struggling to attract new foot traffic and compete with larger bakeries in the area.

The Challenge:

Pain Plaisir's owner, Andrei, knew that his bakery offered a unique and delicious experience, but he was frustrated that it wasn't reaching a wider audience. He recognized that many potential customers were searching online for bakeries in Bucharest, but Pain Plaisir's website was buried deep in search results, often overshadowed by bigger competitors.

The Solution:

Andrei decided to invest in local SEO to improve his bakery's visibility in search results. He partnered with a digital marketing agency that specialized in SEO for small businesses. They began by conducting a thorough SEO audit of Pain Plaisir's website, identifying areas for improvement and opportunities for optimization.

The agency implemented a comprehensive SEO strategy, focusing on the following key areas:

- **Keyword Research:** They identified relevant keywords and phrases that potential customers were searching for, such as "bakery in Bucharest," "best croissants in Bucharest," and "artisan bread near me."
- **On-Page Optimization:** They optimized the bakery's website content, including title tags, meta descriptions, header tags, and image alt text, with these target keywords.
- **Local SEO:** They claimed and optimized Pain Plaisir's Google My Business listing, ensuring that the bakery's

name, address, phone number (NAP), and hours of operation were accurate and consistent across the web.
- **Content Creation:** They created engaging and informative blog posts and articles about Pain Plaisir's products, baking techniques, and the bakery's history and values.
- **Link Building:** They reached out to local food bloggers and publications, securing valuable backlinks to the bakery's website.

The Results:

Within a few months, Pain Plaisir started seeing significant improvements in their search engine rankings. Their website began to appear on the first page of Google for relevant keywords, and their Google My Business listing consistently ranked among the top results for "bakery in Bucharest."

As a result, the bakery experienced a surge in website traffic, phone inquiries, and foot traffic. Customers who had never heard of Pain Plaisir before were now discovering them through online searches. The increase in visibility led to a substantial boost in sales, allowing Andrei to expand his product offerings and hire additional staff.

Key Takeaways:

- Local SEO is a powerful tool for small businesses to increase their visibility in local search results and attract new customers.
- A comprehensive SEO strategy should include keyword research, on-page optimization, local SEO, content creation, and link building.
- By investing in SEO, small businesses can compete with larger competitors and achieve significant growth.

- Measuring and tracking results is crucial for understanding the impact of your SEO efforts and making data-driven decisions.

Pain Plaisir's success story is a testament to the power of local SEO for small businesses. By focusing on providing a high-quality product, optimizing their online presence, and implementing effective SEO strategies, they were able to achieve significant growth and become a beloved local institution.

Social Media Marketing: Connect and Engage

Social media platforms offer a powerful way to connect with your audience, build brand awareness, and drive traffic to your website. However, it's important to choose the right platforms for your business and develop a strategic approach to social media marketing.

Imagine social media as a bustling virtual marketplace where billions of people gather to connect, share information, and discover new products and services. It's a place where you can build relationships with your target audience, showcase your brand's personality, and drive meaningful engagement.

Choosing the Right Platforms: Identifying Your Audience's Preferred Platforms

With so many social media platforms available, it can be overwhelming to decide where to focus your efforts. The key is to choose the platforms where your target audience is most active and engaged.

Here are a few questions to consider:

- **Who is your target audience?** What are their demographics, interests, and online behavior?
- **What are your goals for social media?** Do you want to increase brand awareness, drive website traffic, generate leads, or build a community?
- **What type of content do you want to create?** Are you focusing on text, images, videos, or a combination?
- **What resources do you have available?** Social media marketing can be time-consuming, so consider how much time and resources you can dedicate to each platform.

Once you've answered these questions, you can start narrowing down your choices. Here's a quick overview of some popular social media platforms and their target audiences:

- **Facebook:** The largest social media platform with a diverse user base. Good for reaching a broad audience and building brand awareness.
- **Instagram:** A visual platform popular with younger demographics. Ideal for businesses with visually appealing products or services.
- **Twitter:** A fast-paced platform for sharing news, opinions, and real-time updates. Good for businesses that want to engage in conversations and stay on top of trends.
- **LinkedIn:** A professional networking platform. Ideal for B2B businesses and those looking to connect with industry professionals.
- **Pinterest:** A visual platform for discovering and saving ideas. Good for businesses in the fashion, food, home decor, and DIY industries.
- **TikTok:** A short-form video platform popular with younger

generations. Ideal for businesses with creative and engaging video content.

Quick Tip: Don't try to be on every platform. Instead, focus your efforts on the platforms where you can have the most impact and reach your target audience most effectively.

Social Media Strategies: Building a Community and Driving Engagement

Once you've chosen your platforms, it's time to develop a social media strategy that aligns with your business goals. Here are some key strategies to consider:

- **Create a Content Calendar:** A content calendar helps you plan and schedule your social media posts in advance. This ensures you're posting consistently and that your content is varied and engaging.
- **Share a Mix of Content:** Don't just post promotional content about your products or services. Share a mix of informative, educational, entertaining, and inspirational content that will resonate with your audience.
- **Engage with Your Audience:** Social media is a two-way street. Respond to comments and messages promptly, ask questions, and encourage conversation.
- **Run Contests and Giveaways:** Contests and giveaways can be a fun and effective way to increase engagement and attract new followers.
- **Use Paid Social Media Advertising:** Paid social media advertising allows you to target specific demographics and interests, ensuring your message reaches the right people.
- **Collaborate with Influencers:** Partnering with influencers in your industry can help you reach a wider audience and

build credibility.
- **Track Your Results:** Use social media analytics tools to track your performance and identify what's working and what's not.

Quick Wins for Social Media:

Here are a few quick tips to get started with social media marketing:

- **Optimize Your Profiles:** Make sure your profiles are complete and up-to-date. Use a high-quality profile picture and cover photo that represents your brand.
- **Use High-Quality Visuals:** Images and videos tend to perform better on social media than text-only posts. Use eye-catching visuals that are relevant to your content.
- **Use Hashtags:** Research relevant hashtags to increase the visibility of your posts and reach a wider audience.
- **Post at Optimal Times:** Analyze your audience's activity to determine the best times to post for maximum engagement.
- **Interact with Other Users:** Follow other businesses and influencers in your industry, share their content, and leave thoughtful comments.

Social Media Case Study: "The Style Haven Boutique" Finds Success on Instagram

The Style Haven Boutique, a charming clothing store nestled in the heart of a bustling downtown area, was facing stiff competition from online retailers and larger chain stores. With a limited marketing budget, they needed a cost-effective way to reach their target audience and drive foot traffic to their store.

The Challenge:

The boutique's owner, Olivia, recognized the potential of social media but was unsure how to leverage it effectively. She had created an Instagram account for the store but wasn't seeing much engagement or impact on sales. She needed a strategy to stand out in the crowded fashion landscape and connect with her ideal customers.

The Solution:

Olivia decided to focus her efforts on Instagram, crafting a visually appealing and cohesive brand presence on the platform. She started by curating a beautiful feed, showcasing high-quality photos of her latest arrivals, styled outfits, and behind-the-scenes glimpses of the boutique.

To foster engagement, Olivia implemented several tactics:

- **Interactive Stories:** She used Instagram Stories to share polls, quizzes, and Q&A sessions, encouraging her followers to interact with the brand.
- **Hashtags:** Olivia researched and used relevant hashtags to increase the visibility of her posts and reach a wider audience.
- **Collaborations:** She partnered with local influencers and bloggers, offering them store credit or discounts in exchange for promoting her products.
- **Contests and Giveaways:** Olivia ran regular contests and giveaways, rewarding her followers for engaging with her posts and sharing them with their friends.
- **Shoppable Posts:** She utilized Instagram's shopping feature to make it easy for her followers to purchase products directly from her posts.

The Results:

Olivia's strategic approach to Instagram paid off. Within a few months, her follower count grew exponentially, and she started seeing a significant increase in both online and in-store sales. Customers would often come into the store with screenshots of Instagram posts, ready to purchase the items they had seen.

The Style Haven Boutique's Instagram success can be attributed to several factors:

- **Visually Appealing Content:** The high-quality photos and curated feed created an aesthetically pleasing brand image that resonated with their target audience.
- **Consistent Posting:** By posting regularly and using a content calendar, Olivia ensured her followers were consistently reminded of her brand and its offerings.
- **Interactive Content:** The polls, quizzes, and Q&A sessions in Instagram Stories encouraged engagement and made followers feel more connected to the brand.
- **Influencer Marketing:** Partnering with influencers helped The Style Haven Boutique reach a wider audience and leverage the trust that influencers had built with their followers.
- **Shoppable Posts:** By making it easy for customers to purchase products directly from Instagram, the boutique reduced friction in the buying process and increased sales.

Key Takeaways:

- Instagram can be a powerful tool for small businesses to build brand awareness, connect with customers, and drive sales.
- Creating high-quality, visually appealing content is essen-

tial for success on Instagram.
- Regularly engaging with your audience through interactive content and responding to comments can foster a loyal following.
- Collaborating with influencers and utilizing shoppable posts can significantly boost your reach and sales potential.
- Tracking your Instagram analytics is crucial for measuring your success and identifying areas for improvement.

This case study demonstrates that with a strategic and creative approach, even a small business with a limited budget can achieve significant results on Instagram. By focusing on building a strong brand presence, creating engaging content, and fostering relationships with followers, businesses can tap into the immense potential of this social media platform to drive growth and success.

Email Marketing: Nurture Leads and Drive Sales

While social media is great for building brand awareness and engaging with your audience, email marketing remains one of the most effective channels for driving sales. With email marketing, you can directly reach your subscribers' inboxes with personalized messages and offers.

Building Your Email List:

The first step to successful email marketing is building a high-quality email list. Here are a few ways to do that:

- **Offer a Lead Magnet:** A lead magnet is a free resource that you offer in exchange for an email address. This could be

an e-book, checklist, template, or discount code.
- **Use Opt-in Forms:** Place opt-in forms on your website and social media profiles to encourage visitors to sign up for your email list.
- **Promote Your Email List:** Let people know about your email list and the benefits of subscribing. You can promote it on your website, social media, and in your email signature.

Email Marketing Strategies:

Once you have a list of subscribers, you can start sending them targeted email campaigns. Here are a few effective strategies:

- **Welcome Emails:** Send a series of welcome emails to new subscribers to introduce your brand and build a relationship.
- **Newsletters:** Send regular newsletters with company updates, new product announcements, or helpful tips and resources.
- **Promotional Emails:** Offer exclusive discounts, promotions, or early access to new products to your email subscribers.
- **Abandoned Cart Emails:** Send reminders to customers who have added items to their cart but haven't completed their purchase.
- **Re-engagement Emails:** Try to re-engage inactive subscribers with special offers or personalized content.

Quick Wins for Email Marketing:

- **Personalize Your Emails:** Use your subscribers' names and segment your list based on their interests to send more targeted emails.

- **Use Compelling Subject Lines:** Your subject line is the first thing subscribers will see, so make it catchy and relevant.
- **Keep Your Emails Concise:** Get to the point quickly and avoid overwhelming subscribers with too much information.
- **Test Different Approaches:** Experiment with different types of emails, subject lines, and calls to action to see what works best for your audience.
- **Track Your Results:** Monitor your email open rates, click-through rates, and conversion rates to measure the effectiveness of your campaigns.

Email Marketing Case Study: The Pet Pampering Parlor

The Pet Pampering Parlor, a small grooming salon nestled in a suburban neighborhood, was struggling to retain customers and increase repeat business. They had a loyal following of pet owners who loved their services, but they weren't seeing much repeat business or referrals.

The Challenge:

The salon's owner, Emily, recognized that she needed to find a way to stay connected with her customers and encourage them to return for regular grooming sessions. She knew that email marketing could be a powerful tool, but she wasn't sure where to start.

The Solution:

Emily decided to implement a simple email marketing strategy. She began by offering a "Welcome Back" discount to all new customers who signed up for her email list. This gave them an incentive to provide their email addresses and come back for another visit.

She then started sending out a monthly newsletter to her

subscribers. The newsletter included:

- **Helpful Tips:** Emily shared tips on pet care, grooming, and training, positioning herself as an expert in the field.
- **Promotions and Discounts:** She offered exclusive discounts and promotions to her email subscribers, encouraging them to book appointments.
- **Customer Spotlights:** Emily featured photos and stories of happy customers and their pets, creating a sense of community and connection.

The Results:

Within a few months, Emily noticed a significant increase in repeat business. Her email subscribers were more likely to book regular grooming appointments and refer their friends and family. Her open rates were consistently high, and she received positive feedback from customers who appreciated the valuable information and special offers she provided.

The Pet Pampering Parlor's email marketing campaign was a resounding success. It not only helped Emily retain customers but also increased her brand awareness and generated new leads. By consistently providing value and building relationships with her subscribers, she was able to turn her email list into a loyal customer base.

Key Takeaways:

- Email marketing can be a highly effective tool for small businesses to drive sales and increase customer engagement.
- Offering a lead magnet (like a discount) can help you quickly build your email list.
- Sending regular newsletters with valuable content, promo-

tions, and customer spotlights can help you stay connected with your audience and encourage repeat business.
- Tracking your email metrics (open rates, click-through rates, conversions) is crucial for measuring the success of your campaigns and identifying areas for improvement.

This case study demonstrates that even a simple email marketing strategy can yield significant results for small businesses. By focusing on building relationships with your subscribers and providing them with valuable content and offers, you can turn your email list into a loyal customer base that will support your business for years to come.

By implementing these SEO, social media, and email marketing strategies, you can attract more qualified leads to your website, build stronger relationships with your audience, and ultimately drive more sales for your business.

Content Marketing: Building Relationships Through Valuable Content

In the bustling digital marketplace, content is king. Content marketing involves creating and sharing valuable, relevant, and consistent content to attract and engage your target audience. It's about providing information that helps, educates, or entertains your potential customers, ultimately building trust and driving profitable customer action. Think of it as nurturing a garden: you plant seeds (content), water them (promote), and cultivate them (engage) to eventually harvest the fruits of your labor (leads and sales).

Why Content Marketing Matters for Your Business

- **Attracts and Engages:** High-quality content draws potential customers to your website and social media channels.
- **Builds Trust and Credibility:** By offering valuable information, you position yourself as an expert in your industry.
- **Improves SEO:** Search engines favor websites with fresh, relevant content, leading to better rankings and more organic traffic.
- **Nurtures Leads:** Content can guide potential customers through the buying process, turning them from curious visitors into loyal customers.
- **Cost-Effective:** Content marketing is often more affordable than traditional advertising and can provide a higher return on investment (ROI).

Types of Content: Variety is the Spice of Digital Marketing

There are countless types of content you can create, each with its own strengths and benefits:

- **Blog Posts:** Share your expertise, industry insights, or company updates.
- **Articles:** Publish in-depth articles on topics relevant to your audience.
- **Videos:** Create tutorials, product demos, or behind-the-scenes glimpses.
- **Infographics:** Present complex information in a visually appealing format.
- **Podcasts:** Share interviews, discussions, or audio content on relevant topics.
- **Social Media Posts:** Short, engaging updates to connect with your audience.
- **eBooks and Guides:** Offer in-depth, downloadable re-

sources on specific topics.

The best types of content for your business will depend on your target audience, your goals, and your available resources.

Creating a Content Calendar: Planning for Success

A content calendar is a schedule that outlines what content you'll create, when you'll publish it, and on which channels. It helps you stay organized, maintain consistency, and ensure that your content aligns with your overall marketing strategy.

Your content calendar should include:

- **Content Type:** Blog post, video, social media post, etc.
- **Topic:** The subject of your content.
- **Publish Date:** When the content will be published.
- **Channel:** Where the content will be shared (e.g., website, Facebook, LinkedIn).
- **Author/Owner:** The person responsible for creating and publishing the content.

Quick Wins for Content Marketing:

- **Repurpose Content:** Turn a blog post into a video or social media graphics to maximize its reach.
- **Promote Your Content:** Share your content on social media, email newsletters, and other relevant channels.
- **Guest Blog:** Write guest posts for other websites to expand your reach and build backlinks.
- **Measure Your Results:** Track your content's performance using analytics tools to see what's resonating with your audience and adjust your strategy accordingly.

Content Marketing Case Study: Pain Plaisir Bakery Engages Customers with Delicious Content

In addition to their SEO efforts (mentioned earlier), Pain Plaisir Bakery wanted to further engage their growing online audience and build a loyal community around their brand. They recognized that content marketing could be a powerful tool for achieving this goal.

The Challenge:

While Pain Plaisir had a beautiful website and a growing social media presence, they weren't sure what type of content would resonate most with their audience. They also needed a way to create and share content consistently without overwhelming their small team.

The Solution:

Pain Plaisir developed a content marketing strategy that focused on providing value to their customers and showcasing their passion for baking. They started by creating a blog on their website, where they shared:

- **Recipes:** They published delicious recipes for some of their most popular pastries and bread, encouraging customers to try baking at home.
- **Behind-the-Scenes Stories:** They shared stories about the bakery's history, their team of bakers, and the ingredients they use, giving customers a glimpse into the heart of their business.
- **Baking Tips and Tutorials:** They offered helpful tips and tutorials on baking techniques, ingredient substitutions, and seasonal recipes.
- **Customer Spotlights:** They featured stories and photos of satisfied customers enjoying their Pain Plaisir treats,

creating a sense of community and connection.

To ensure consistency, Pain Plaisir created a content calendar that outlined what content they would create, when they would publish it, and on which channels. They promoted their content on social media, in their email newsletters, and through partnerships with local food bloggers.

The Results:

Pain Plaisir's content marketing efforts paid off handsomely. Their blog became a go-to resource for baking enthusiasts in Bucharest, and their social media engagement soared. Customers loved the recipes, stories, and tips, and they eagerly shared the content with their friends and family.

The bakery's email list grew rapidly, as people signed up to receive their newsletters and get access to exclusive recipes and promotions. This increased engagement led to more website traffic, foot traffic, and ultimately, a significant boost in sales.

Key Takeaways:

- Content marketing can be a powerful tool for small businesses to engage with their audience, build brand awareness, and drive sales.
- Creating valuable and relevant content is key to attracting and retaining customers.
- Sharing a variety of content types, such as recipes, stories, and tutorials, can appeal to a wider audience.
- A content calendar helps you stay organized and consistent with your content creation and promotion.
- Promoting your content through various channels can maximize its reach and impact.

Pain Plaisir's success story demonstrates the power of content marketing to connect with customers on a deeper level and create a loyal following. By consistently providing valuable content, they were able to transform their bakery from a hidden gem into a thriving local business.

Paid Advertising: Reaching New Heights with Targeted Ads

While organic marketing strategies like SEO and content marketing are essential for long-term growth, paid advertising offers a way to accelerate your results and reach a wider audience quickly. Paid advertising involves paying to display your ads on various platforms, such as search engines, social media, and websites.

Paid advertising acts as a megaphone, amplifying your message and enabling you to target specific demographics, interests, and behaviors.. It's a powerful tool for generating leads, driving sales, and increasing brand awareness.

Introduction to Paid Advertising

Paid advertising, also known as pay-per-click (PPC) advertising, is a digital marketing model where advertisers pay a fee each time one of their ads is clicked. It's a way to buy visits to your site, rather than attempting to "earn" those visits organically.

Types of Paid Advertising

- **Search Engine Advertising (SEA):** Ads that appear at the top of search engine results pages (SERPs) when users search for specific keywords. Google Ads is the most popular SEA platform.
- **Social Media Advertising:** Ads that appear on social media platforms like Facebook, Instagram, Twitter, and LinkedIn.

You can target users based on their interests, demographics, and behavior.
- **Display Advertising:** Ads that appear on websites and apps that are part of a display network. These ads can be targeted based on various factors, including demographics, interests, and browsing behavior.
- **Retargeting:** Ads that are shown to people who have previously visited your website or interacted with your brand online. This can be a highly effective way to re-engage potential customers and bring them back to your site.

Choosing the Right Platforms: Where Your Ideal Customers Click

The key to successful paid advertising is choosing the right platforms for your business. Consider the following factors:

- **Your Target Audience:** Which platforms does your target audience use most frequently?
- **Your Budget:** Paid advertising can range from very affordable to quite expensive, depending on the platform and your targeting options. Set a realistic budget and choose platforms that fit your financial resources.
- **Your Goals:** What are you hoping to achieve with paid advertising? Do you want to increase brand awareness, generate leads, or drive sales? Different platforms may be better suited for different goals.

Setting Up and Managing Campaigns: A Step-by-Step Guide

Setting up and managing paid advertising campaigns can seem daunting, but with the right approach, it can be quite simple. Here's a basic step-by-step guide:

1. **Set Your Goals:** What do you want to achieve with your campaign?
2. **Define Your Target Audience:** Who are you trying to reach?
3. **Choose Your Platform(s):** Which platforms are best suited for your target audience and goals?
4. **Create Your Ads:** Write compelling ad copy and design eye-catching visuals.
5. **Set Your Budget and Bids:** Determine how much you're willing to spend and how much you're willing to pay per click or impression.
6. **Monitor and Optimize:** Track your campaign's performance and make adjustments as needed.

Quick Wins for Paid Advertising:

- **Start Small:** Begin with a small budget and test different ad formats, targeting options, and platforms to see what works best for you.
- **Use Relevant Keywords:** If you're running search engine ads, use keywords that your target audience is searching for.
- **Create Compelling Ads:** Write ad copy that grabs attention and highlights the benefits of your product or service.
- **Use High-Quality Visuals:** Use eye-catching images or videos that are relevant to your ad and target audience.
- **Track Your Results:** Monitor your campaign's performance and make adjustments as needed to improve your ROI.

Paid Advertising Case Study: From Clicks to Conversions – Bloom & Wild's Facebook Ads Triumph

Bloom & Wild, a budding online flower delivery service, was

eager to expand its reach beyond its existing customer base and increase sales. They recognized the potential of Facebook Ads to target specific demographics and interests, but they were unsure how to create effective campaigns that would drive results.

The Challenge:
Bloom & Wild faced several challenges:

- **Limited Brand Awareness:** They were a relatively new company and needed to increase their visibility among their target audience.
- **Competitive Market:** The online flower delivery market was saturated with established players, making it difficult to stand out.
- **Seasonal Fluctuations:** Their sales were heavily dependent on holidays and special occasions, leading to inconsistent revenue throughout the year.

The Solution:
Bloom & Wild partnered with a digital marketing agency to develop a comprehensive Facebook Ads strategy. The agency's approach focused on:

- **Audience Targeting:** They meticulously defined Bloom & Wild's target audience, identifying demographics (age, gender, location), interests (gardening, home decor, gifts), and behaviors (engaged couples, people celebrating birthdays).
- **Compelling Ad Creatives:** They designed visually striking ads featuring high-quality images of Bloom & Wild's unique bouquets and arrangements. The ad copy highlighted the company's commitment to quality, sustainability, and

exceptional customer service.
- **Retargeting Campaigns:** They implemented retargeting campaigns to re-engage users who had previously visited the website or added items to their cart but didn't complete a purchase.
- **A/B Testing:** They continuously tested different ad variations, targeting options, and bidding strategies to optimize campaign performance.
- **Seasonal Campaigns:** They created targeted campaigns for holidays and special occasions, offering exclusive discounts and promotions to drive sales during peak periods.

The Results:

Bloom & Wild's Facebook Ads campaigns yielded impressive results:

- **Increased Website Traffic:** Their website traffic increased by 45% within the first three months of running the ads.
- **Higher Conversion Rates:** The targeted ads led to a 20% increase in online orders.
- **Improved Brand Awareness:** The brand's reach expanded significantly, with a 30% increase in Facebook followers.
- **Reduced Customer Acquisition Costs:** By optimizing their campaigns, Bloom & Wild was able to lower their cost per acquisition, making their marketing efforts more cost-effective.
- **Smoother Seasonal Sales:** The targeted seasonal campaigns helped to reduce the impact of sales fluctuations and generate more consistent revenue throughout the year.

Key Takeaways:

- Facebook Ads can be a highly effective tool for e-commerce businesses to increase brand awareness, drive traffic, and boost sales.
- Precise audience targeting is crucial for reaching the right people with the right message.
- Compelling ad creatives and copy can significantly impact click-through and conversion rates.
- Retargeting campaigns can be a powerful way to re-engage potential customers and recover abandoned carts.
- Continuous testing and optimization are essential for maximizing the ROI of your Facebook Ads campaigns.

Bloom & Wild's success story demonstrates the potential of Facebook Ads to transform a small e-commerce business into a thriving online brand. By understanding their target audience, creating compelling ads, and continuously optimizing their campaigns, they were able to achieve significant growth and establish themselves as a leader in the online flower delivery market.

Additional Quick Wins for SEO, Social Media, and Content Marketing:

In addition to the quick wins we've already discussed, here are a few more tips to boost your digital marketing efforts:
SEO:

- **Optimize for Voice Search:** As voice search becomes more popular, optimize your content for voice queries by using natural language and long-tail keywords.

- **Improve Website Speed:** A slow website can negatively impact your search engine rankings and user experience. Use tools like Google PageSpeed Insights to identify areas for improvement.
- **Use Internal Linking:** Link to other relevant pages within your website to help users navigate your site and improve your SEO.

Social Media:

- **Use Social Media Analytics Tools:** Track your social media performance and gain insights into your audience's behavior with tools like Hootsuite Insights or Sprout Social.
- **Run Social Media Contests:** Contests and giveaways can increase engagement and generate excitement around your brand.
- **Engage in Live Video:** Live video is a great way to connect with your audience in real-time and build a stronger relationship.

Content Marketing:

- **Repurpose Content:** Turn your blog posts into videos, infographics, or social media posts to reach a wider audience and extend the lifespan of your content.
- **Use User-Generated Content:** Encourage your customers to create and share content related to your brand. This can help you build trust and authenticity.
- **Collaborate with Other Businesses:** Partner with other businesses in your industry to create co-branded content and reach a wider audience.

Tools and Resources

To help you implement these strategies, here's a list of recommended tools and resources:

SEO Tools:

- **Google Search Console:** A free tool from Google that helps you monitor your website's performance in search results.
- **SEMrush:** A comprehensive SEO tool that provides keyword research, competitor analysis, site audit, and more.
- **Ahrefs:** Another powerful SEO tool that offers similar features to SEMrush.
- **Yoast SEO:** A popular WordPress plugin that helps you optimize your website content for search engines.

Social Media Tools:

- **Hootsuite:** A social media management platform that allows you to schedule posts, monitor your mentions, and track your performance.
- **Buffer:** A social media scheduling tool that helps you maintain a consistent posting schedule.
- **Sprout Social:** A social media management platform that offers a range of features, including listening, publishing, engagement, and analytics.

Content Marketing Tools:

- **Buzzsumo:** A tool that helps you find trending content and influencers in your industry.
- **CoSchedule:** A marketing calendar that helps you plan,

organize, and promote your content.
- **Canva:** A graphic design tool that makes it easy to create professional-looking images for your website and social media.

Paid Advertising Tools:

- **Google Ads Editor:** A desktop application that makes it easier to manage large Google Ads campaigns.
- **Facebook Ads Manager:** The platform for creating and managing Facebook and Instagram advertising campaigns.

Additional Resources:

- **Moz Blog:** A great resource for learning about SEO and digital marketing.
- **Neil Patel:** A renowned digital marketing expert who shares valuable insights on his blog and YouTube channel.
- **Social Media Examiner:** A website dedicated to providing social media marketing tips and resources.

By utilizing these tools and resources, you'll be well-equipped to implement effective digital marketing strategies and achieve your business goals.

5

Creating Content That Converts

Content marketing is a powerful tool that can transform your website from a static brochure into a dynamic hub for attracting, engaging, and converting customers. By providing valuable information, building trust, and establishing yourself as an authority in your industry, you can turn casual visitors into loyal customers and brand advocates.

Crafting Your Content Strategy: A Roadmap for Success

A well-defined content strategy is the cornerstone of effective content marketing. It serves as a roadmap, guiding your efforts and ensuring that your content aligns with your overall business objectives.

To create a winning content strategy, start by asking yourself these key questions:

1. **What are your goals?** Are you looking to increase brand awareness, generate leads, drive sales, or establish thought leadership? Clearly defining your goals will help

you focus your efforts and measure your success.
2. **Who is your target audience?** What are their interests, needs, and pain points? Understanding your audience is crucial for creating content that resonates with them and provides value.
3. **What key messages do you want to convey?** What unique perspective or expertise can you offer? Clearly articulating your key messages will help you craft content that sets you apart from the competition.
4. **What types of content will you create?** Will you focus on blog posts, articles, videos, infographics, or other formats? Choose the types of content that best align with your audience's preferences and your resources.
5. **Which channels will you use to distribute your content?** Will you publish on your website, social media, email, or other platforms? Consider where your audience spends their time online and tailor your distribution strategy accordingly.
6. **How will you measure the success of your content?** What metrics will you track to gauge the effectiveness of your content marketing efforts? Common metrics include website traffic, social media engagement, lead generation, and sales.

Content Creation: Types of Content That Resonate

There's no one-size-fits-all approach to content marketing. The best type of content for your business will depend on your target audience, your goals, and your available resources. Here are a few popular and effective content formats:

- **Blog Posts:** Share your expertise, industry insights, or company news in a conversational and informative tone. Keep your blog posts concise, focused on a single topic, and use catchy headlines and visuals to attract readers. *Example: "5 Tips for Choosing the Perfect Coffee Beans"*
- **Articles:** Dive deeper into specific topics with in-depth articles that showcase your thought leadership. Publish your articles on your website or contribute to industry publications to reach a wider audience. *Example: "The History of Coffee: From Ancient Ethiopia to Your Cup"*
- **Videos:** Create engaging videos that demonstrate your products or services, tell your brand story, or educate your audience. Share your videos on platforms like YouTube, social media, and your website. *Example: "How to Brew the Perfect Cup of Coffee at Home"*
- **Infographics:** Use visuals to present complex information in a simple and easy-to-understand format. Infographics are highly shareable and can help you reach a wider audience. *Example: "The Anatomy of a Coffee Bean"*
- **Podcasts:** Share interviews, discussions, or audio content on topics relevant to your audience. Podcasts are a convenient way for people to consume content while on the go. *Example: "The Coffee Connoisseur Podcast"*
- **Social Media Posts:** Create short, attention-grabbing posts that promote your content and engage your followers. Use visuals, hashtags, and calls to action to encourage interaction. *Example: "Tag a friend who needs this coffee in their life!"*
- **eBooks and Guides:** Offer in-depth, downloadable re-

sources that provide valuable information and generate leads. Gated content like ebooks can be used to collect email addresses and build your subscriber list. *Example: "The Ultimate Guide to Coffee Brewing"*

Remember, the key is to create high-quality content that is relevant, informative, and engaging for your target audience.

Promoting Your Content: Getting Your Message Out There

Creating great content is only half the battle. You also need to get your message out there and attract your target audience. Think of it like baking a delicious cake – it won't do you much good if no one knows it exists! Here are a few effective content promotion strategies:

- **Social Media Sharing:** Share your content on social media platforms like Facebook, Twitter, LinkedIn, and Instagram. Use relevant hashtags, eye-catching visuals, and compelling captions to increase engagement. Tailor your message to each platform and consider paid promotion options to reach a wider audience. For example, use eye-catching visuals and a catchy caption like "New blog post alert! Learn how to brew the perfect cup of coffee at home. Click the link in our bio to read more." on Instagram.
- **Email Marketing:** Send email newsletters to your subscribers with links to your latest content. Segment your list based on interests and tailor your emails accordingly. Personalize your emails with the recipient's name and use strong subject lines to entice them to open. For example, your subject line could be "Don't miss our latest coffee

brewing tips!"
- **Paid Advertising:** Invest in paid advertising campaigns on platforms like Google Ads and social media to amplify your reach and target specific demographics. Consider running search ads, display ads, or social media ads to promote your content to a broader audience. For example, target coffee lovers in your local area with a Facebook ad promoting your new coffee brewing guide.
- **Influencer Marketing:** Partner with influencers in your industry to share your content with their followers. This can help you tap into new audiences and gain credibility through association with trusted figures. For example, collaborate with a popular food blogger to create a recipe featuring your coffee beans.
- **Community Engagement:** Participate in online forums, groups, and communities related to your industry. Share your expertise, answer questions, and build relationships with potential customers. By actively engaging in these communities, you can establish yourself as a thought leader and drive traffic to your website. For example, answer questions about coffee brewing in a coffee lovers forum or group.

The Art of Storytelling: Making Your Brand Relatable

Stories are powerful tools for connecting with your audience on an emotional level. By sharing your brand's story, you can humanize your business and make it more relatable. Think about the challenges you've overcome, the values that drive you, and the unique experiences that have shaped your brand.

Here are a few ways to incorporate storytelling into your

content:

- **Share Your Origin Story:** How did your business come to be? What inspired you to start it? What obstacles did you overcome?
- **Highlight Customer Success Stories:** Share testimonials and case studies of how your products or services have helped your customers achieve their goals.
- **Showcase Your Team:** Introduce the people behind your brand. Share their stories, passions, and expertise.
- **Use a Conversational Tone:** Write in a friendly and approachable way, as if you're talking to a friend.
- **Incorporate Humor and Emotion:** Don't be afraid to inject some personality into your content. Make people laugh, cry, or feel inspired.

Remember, people connect with stories. By sharing yours, you can create a deeper connection with your audience and make your brand more memorable.

Measuring Content Success: Tracking Your ROI

Creating and promoting content is just the beginning. To truly succeed with content marketing, you need to measure its effectiveness and continuously optimize your strategy.

Here are some key metrics to track:

- **Website Traffic:** How much traffic is your content driving to your website? Use tools like Google Analytics to track the number of visitors, page views, and bounce rate. This will help you understand which content is performing best and

where you need to improve.
- **Engagement:** How many likes, shares, comments, and other interactions is your content receiving on social media? Track these metrics using the analytics tools provided by each platform. This can give you insights into what type of content resonates most with your audience.
- **Lead Generation:** How many leads is your content generating through downloads, signups, or contact forms? Use tracking links and lead capture forms to measure this. This will help you assess the effectiveness of your lead generation efforts.
- **Sales:** What impact is your content having on your sales revenue? Track the number of sales generated from specific pieces of content or campaigns. This is the ultimate measure of your content marketing success.
- **Brand Awareness:** Are you seeing an increase in brand mentions or social media sentiment? Use social listening tools to monitor conversations about your brand online. This can help you gauge the impact of your content on brand perception.

By tracking these metrics and analyzing your results, you can identify which types of content are performing best, which channels are driving the most traffic, and which strategies are generating the most leads and sales. This data will allow you to refine your content strategy and make data-driven decisions to improve your results over time.

Social Listening: Hear What Your Customers Are Saying

Social media isn't just about broadcasting your own message; it's also a powerful listening tool. Social listening involves monitoring social media platforms for mentions of your brand, products, competitors, or industry keywords. This valuable feedback loop allows you to:

- **Understand Your Audience:** Get a real-time pulse on what your customers and potential customers are saying about your brand, products, or industry.
- **Identify Trends:** Spot emerging trends and conversations that could impact your business.
- **Manage Your Reputation:** Quickly address negative comments or reviews and mitigate potential crises.
- **Find Opportunities:** Discover new product ideas, marketing strategies, or partnership opportunities.

How to Use Social Listening Tools: Tune In to the Conversation

Several tools can help you monitor and analyze social media conversations:

- **Hootsuite:** This social media management platform offers powerful social listening features, allowing you to track mentions of your brand, keywords, and competitors across multiple platforms.
- **Mention:** This tool monitors mentions of your brand across the web and social media, providing real-time alerts and sentiment analysis.
- **Brandwatch:** This comprehensive social listening platform

offers advanced features like trend analysis, image recognition, and competitor benchmarking.
- **BuzzSumo:** While primarily a content discovery tool, BuzzSumo also offers social listening capabilities, allowing you to track mentions and analyze the performance of your content on social media.

Quick Tips for Social Listening:

- **Define Your Keywords:** Identify the keywords and phrases you want to track, such as your brand name, product names, or industry-specific terms.
- **Set Up Alerts:** Most social listening tools allow you to set up alerts so you're notified whenever your brand or keywords are mentioned.
- **Analyze Sentiment:** Monitor the sentiment of conversations about your brand to understand how people feel about you.
- **Engage with Your Audience:** Respond to comments and questions promptly and professionally.
- **Track Your Progress:** Use social listening data to track your brand's reputation over time and measure the impact of your marketing campaigns.

Social Listening Case Study: Hotel Chain Responds to Negative Feedback and Improves Customer Experience

A luxury hotel chain received several negative reviews on social media about the slow service at one of its restaurants. By using a social listening tool, they were able to quickly identify the issue and respond to the dissatisfied customers, offering apologies and complimentary meals. They also used the feedback to improve their restaurant's service, leading to a significant increase in positive reviews and customer satisfaction.

Important Note: Social listening is not just about reacting to negative feedback. It's also about identifying opportunities to connect with your audience, build relationships, and improve your products or services.

Incorporating social listening into your content marketing strategy can help you stay ahead of the curve, gain valuable insights into your audience, and ultimately build a stronger brand.

6

Paid Advertising Demystified: Your Fast Track to Growth

While organic marketing strategies like SEO and content marketing are essential for long-term brand building, paid advertising offers a powerful way to accelerate your results and reach a wider audience quickly. In this chapter, we'll demystify paid advertising, guiding you through the key platforms and strategies so you can confidently invest your marketing budget and achieve your business goals.

Unleashing the Power of Paid Advertising

Paid advertising, also known as pay-per-click (PPC) advertising, is a digital marketing model where you pay a fee each time one of your ads is clicked. It's a direct way to buy visibility and drive traffic to your website, unlike organic methods that rely on earning views over time.

Think of paid advertising as a spotlight that shines directly on your business, ensuring your message is seen by the right people at the right time. It's a versatile tool that can be used to:

- **Generate leads:** Attract potential customers who are actively searching for products or services like yours.
- **Boost website traffic:** Drive targeted traffic to your website and increase brand awareness.
- **Increase sales:** Encourage immediate action from potential customers by promoting special offers or discounts.
- **Remarket to previous visitors:** Reach people who have already shown an interest in your business and bring them back to your website.

Choosing Your Paid Advertising Arsenal: Key Platforms and Strategies

The world of paid advertising offers a diverse range of platforms and strategies to suit different budgets and goals. Let's explore some of the most popular options:

Search Engine Advertising (SEA): Dominating the Search Results

When potential customers search for products or services online, they often turn to search engines like Google or Bing. Search engine advertising allows you to display your ads at the top of search results pages (SERPs) when users search for specific keywords relevant to your business.

- **Google Ads:** The most popular SEA platform, Google Ads offers a variety of ad formats, including text ads, shopping ads, and display ads. It allows you to target specific keywords, demographics, locations, and even devices.
- **Microsoft Advertising:** Formerly Bing Ads, Microsoft Advertising allows you to reach a different audience than Google Ads and can be a cost-effective option for some

businesses.

Social Media Advertising: Building Brand Awareness and Engagement

Social media platforms like Facebook, Instagram, Twitter, LinkedIn, and Pinterest offer powerful advertising tools that can help you reach a massive audience and target users based on their interests, demographics, and behavior.

- **Facebook Ads:** With over 2 billion active users, Facebook offers unparalleled reach and targeting options. You can create highly customized ads that appear in users' news feeds, sidebars, and even within Messenger.
- **Instagram Ads:** Instagram is a visual platform that's ideal for businesses with visually appealing products or services. You can create eye-catching image and video ads that appear in users' feeds and Stories.
- **Twitter Ads:** Promote your tweets or create custom ads to reach a specific audience on Twitter. You can target users based on their interests, followers, or even the hashtags they use.
- **LinkedIn Ads:** If you're a B2B business, LinkedIn Ads can be a highly effective way to reach decision-makers and professionals in your industry.
- **Pinterest Ads:** Pinterest is a visual discovery platform where users go to find inspiration and ideas. Promoted pins can help you reach a targeted audience interested in your products or services.

Display Advertising: Expanding Your Reach Across the Web

Display advertising involves placing banner ads or other visual ads on websites and apps that are part of a display network. This allows you to reach a wide audience across different platforms and websites.

- **Google Display Network:** Google's vast network of websites and apps offers a wide range of targeting options, allowing you to reach users based on their interests, demographics, and browsing behavior.
- **Programmatic Advertising:** This automated buying and selling of ad inventory allows you to target specific audiences in real-time, optimizing your campaigns for maximum efficiency and ROI.

Retargeting/Remarketing: Reconnect with Past Visitors

Retargeting, also known as remarketing, is a powerful strategy that allows you to show ads to people who have previously visited your website or interacted with your brand online. This can be a highly effective way to stay top-of-mind and bring them back to your site to complete a purchase.

- **Pixel-Based Retargeting:** This involves placing a small piece of code (a pixel) on your website. When someone visits your site, the pixel drops a cookie on their browser, allowing you to show them targeted ads as they browse other websites.
- **List-Based Retargeting:** This involves uploading a list of email addresses or phone numbers to a platform like Facebook or Google Ads. You can then show ads specifically to those people.

Creating Effective Paid Advertising Campaigns: A Step-by-Step Guide

Now that you understand the different types of paid advertising, let's explore how to create and manage effective campaigns that deliver results. Remember, successful paid advertising requires a strategic approach and continuous optimization.

1. **Set Clear Goals:**

- **Define Your Objectives:** What do you want to achieve with your paid advertising campaigns? Are you looking to increase website traffic, generate leads, boost sales, or improve brand awareness?
- **Set SMART Goals:** Make sure your goals are Specific, Measurable, Achievable, Relevant, and Time-bound. For example, instead of saying "I want to increase website traffic," you could set a goal to "Increase website traffic by 20% within three months."

2. **Define Your Target Audience:**

- **Identify Your Ideal Customers:** Who are you trying to reach with your ads? What are their demographics (age, gender, location, income level), interests, and behaviors?
- **Create Buyer Personas:** Develop detailed profiles of your ideal customers, including their pain points, goals, and online behavior.
- **Use Targeting Options:** Most paid advertising platforms offer a wide range of targeting options, such as:
- **Demographic Targeting:** Age, gender, location, language, income level.

- **Interest-Based Targeting:** Interests, hobbies, behaviors.
- **Custom Audiences:** People who have previously interacted with your business (e.g., website visitors, email subscribers, social media followers).
- **Lookalike Audiences:** People who share similar characteristics with your existing customers.
- **Behavioral Targeting:** Based on people's online activities and purchase history.

3. Choose Your Platform(s):

- **Consider Your Audience and Goals:** Select the platforms where your target audience is most active and that align with your campaign goals.
- **Research Platform Costs:** Understand the average cost per click (CPC) or cost per thousand impressions (CPM) on each platform and factor that into your budget.
- **Experiment with Different Platforms:** Don't be afraid to try different platforms to see which ones work best for your business.

4. Craft Compelling Ads:

- **Write Clear and Persuasive Ad Copy:** Highlight the unique benefits of your product or service and create a sense of urgency or exclusivity. Use a strong call to action (CTA) that encourages users to click, such as "Shop Now," "Learn More," or "Get Your Free Quote."
- **Design Eye-Catching Visuals:** Use high-quality images or videos that are relevant to your message and target audience. Keep your visuals simple, visually appealing, and attention-

grabbing.
- **Use A/B Testing:** Create multiple versions of your ads and test them to see which ones perform best. Test different headlines, images, CTAs, and ad formats to optimize your results.

5. Understand Campaign Structure:

- **Campaigns:** The highest level of organization in a paid advertising account. Each campaign has its own budget and settings.
- **Ad Groups:** A collection of ads that share similar targets and placements. Each ad group within a campaign has its own keywords, bids, and ad copy.
- **Keywords:** The words or phrases that you bid on in search engine advertising.
- **Ads:** The individual advertisements that you create and display on the platform.

6. Set Your Budget and Bids:

- **Determine Your Overall Budget:** Decide how much you're willing to spend on paid advertising each month or for a specific campaign.
- **Allocate Your Budget:** Divide your budget across different platforms and campaigns based on your goals and expected ROI.
- **Set Your Bids:** Choose a bidding strategy that aligns with your goals and budget.

7. Monitor and Optimize:

- **Track Your Results:** Use the analytics tools provided by each platform to track your campaign performance. Monitor key metrics like impressions, clicks, click-through rate (CTR), conversions, and return on investment (ROI).
- **Analyze Data:** Identify trends and patterns in your data to understand what's working and what's not. Which ads are performing best? Which keywords are driving the most traffic and conversions? Which demographics are responding best to your ads?
- **Make Adjustments:** Based on your analysis, make adjustments to your campaigns to improve performance. This could involve tweaking your ad copy, changing your targeting options, adjusting your bids, or reallocating your budget.

Setting Realistic Expectations: The Path to Paid Advertising Success

Paid advertising is not a magic bullet, and it's important to set realistic expectations. It takes time, experimentation, and continuous optimization to see significant results. Don't expect overnight success or instant ROI. Instead, focus on building sustainable campaigns that deliver consistent results over time.

Think of paid advertising as a long-term investment, not a quick fix. It's about building relationships with potential customers, increasing brand awareness, and ultimately driving conversions. By setting realistic goals, tracking your progress, and making data-driven decisions, you can maximize the impact of your paid advertising efforts and achieve long-term success.

Landing Page Optimization: The Gateway to Conversions

When someone clicks on your ad, they are directed to a specific page on your website known as the landing page. The landing page is where the magic happens – it's where you have the opportunity to convert visitors into customers or leads.

A well-optimized landing page should:

- **Align with Your Ad:** The landing page should match the message and offer presented in your ad. If your ad promises a free eBook, the landing page should make it easy for visitors to download that eBook.
- **Be Relevant to Your Target Audience:** The content on the landing page should speak directly to the needs and interests of the people who clicked on your ad.
- **Have a Clear Call to Action:** Tell visitors what you want them to do (e.g., "Shop Now," "Sign Up," "Get a Free Quote"). Make your CTA prominent and easy to find.
- **Be Visually Appealing:** Use high-quality images or videos and a clean, uncluttered design.
- **Be Mobile-Friendly:** Ensure your landing page is optimized for mobile devices so that it looks and functions well on smaller screens.

By optimizing your landing pages, you can significantly increase your conversion rates and maximize the ROI of your paid advertising campaigns.

Budgeting Tips: Making the Most of Your Marketing Dollars

Setting a budget for paid advertising can be challenging, especially for small businesses with limited resources. Here are a few tips to help you make the most of your marketing dollars:

- **Start Small:** Begin with a small budget and gradually increase it as you see results. This allows you to test different strategies and platforms without overspending.
- **Set a Daily or Monthly Limit:** Most advertising platforms allow you to set a daily or monthly spending limit to prevent overspending.
- **Focus on Your Most Profitable Products or Services:** Allocate more of your budget to promoting products or services with the highest profit margins.
- **Track Your Spending:** Monitor your ad spending closely and analyze your results to identify which campaigns are most effective.
- **Consider Hiring a Professional:** If you're not sure how to manage your paid advertising budget effectively, consider hiring a digital marketing agency or consultant who can help you optimize your campaigns and get the best possible results.

Remember, paid advertising is an investment, not an expense. By tracking your results and making data-driven decisions, you can ensure that your ad spend is generating a positive return on investment.

Measuring ROI: The Key to Paid Advertising Success

Measuring the return on investment (ROI) of your paid advertising campaigns is essential for understanding their effectiveness and making informed decisions about your marketing strategy.

Here's how to calculate ROI for a paid advertising campaign:

1. **Track Your Conversions:** Set up conversion tracking in your advertising platform (e.g., Google Ads, Facebook Ads) to track the number of desired actions (e.g., purchases, signups, phone calls) that result from your ads.
2. **Calculate Your Cost Per Acquisition (CPA):** Divide your total ad spend by the number of conversions to determine your CPA. This is the average amount you're spending to acquire each new customer or lead.
3. **Determine Your Customer Lifetime Value (CLV):** Estimate the average revenue you generate from each customer over their lifetime. This can be calculated by analyzing your sales data and customer retention rates.
4. **Calculate Your ROI:** Subtract your CPA from your CLV to determine your net profit per customer. Divide this number by your CPA and multiply by 100 to calculate your ROI as a percentage.

For example, if your CPA is $10 and your CLV is $100, your net profit per customer is $90. Your ROI would then be 900% ($90/$10 x 100).

Important Note: ROI isn't always immediate. Some campaigns may take time to generate results, especially if you're focused on brand awareness or long-term customer relationships.

Common Mistakes to Avoid: Navigating the Paid Advertising Pitfalls

Paid advertising can be a powerful tool, but it's important to avoid common mistakes that can waste your budget and hinder your results. Here are a few pitfalls to watch out for:

- **Poor Targeting:** One of the biggest mistakes businesses make with paid advertising is targeting the wrong audience. Make sure you're targeting people who are likely to be interested in your products or services.
- **Irrelevant Ad Creatives:** Your ads should be visually appealing and relevant to your target audience. Avoid using generic or stock photos. Instead, use high-quality images or videos that showcase your products or services in the best possible light.
- **Weak Ad Copy:** Your ad copy should be clear, concise, and persuasive. Highlight the benefits of your product or service and use a strong call to action.
- **Neglecting to Track Results:** If you don't track your campaign performance, you won't know what's working and what's not. Use analytics tools to monitor your results and make data-driven decisions.
- **Not Optimizing Your Campaigns:** Paid advertising requires ongoing optimization. Regularly review your campaign performance and make adjustments to your targeting, bidding, and ad creatives to improve your results.

By avoiding these common mistakes and implementing best practices, you can maximize the effectiveness of your paid advertising campaigns and achieve significant ROI.

Google Consent Mode v2: Navigating the Changing Landscape of Data Privacy

As data privacy regulations become more stringent, businesses must adapt their advertising strategies to ensure compliance and maintain user trust. Google Consent Mode v2 is a tool designed to help businesses navigate this changing landscape while still gathering valuable data for their campaigns.

What is Google Consent Mode v2?

Consent Mode v2 is an update to Google's existing Consent Mode, which allows websites to adjust how Google tags (like those used for Google Ads and Analytics) behave based on users' cookie consent preferences. This means you can respect user privacy choices while still collecting valuable data to inform your marketing efforts.

How Does Consent Mode v2 Affect Paid Advertising?

With Consent Mode v2, the data you can collect will depend on the user's consent preferences. This may impact your paid advertising campaigns in a few ways:

- **Audience Targeting:** If users decline certain types of cookies, you may have less granular data for targeting your ads. However, Google is developing modeling techniques to help fill in the gaps and ensure your campaigns remain effective.
- **Conversion Tracking:** Some conversions may not be tracked if users don't consent to tracking. This could make it harder to measure the success of your campaigns and calculate your return on investment (ROAS).
- **Remarketing:** Remarketing campaigns, which target users who have previously interacted with your website or ads, may be impacted if users decline certain types of cookies.

Strategies for Adapting to Consent Mode v2:

While Consent Mode v2 presents some challenges, there are strategies you can implement to ensure your paid advertising campaigns remain effective and compliant:

- **Prioritize First-Party Data:** Focus on collecting first-party data (data you collect directly from your customers) through email signups, surveys, and other methods. This data is not affected by cookie consent restrictions and can be used to create highly targeted campaigns.
- **Utilize Contextual Targeting:** Contextual targeting allows you to display ads based on the content of a website or app, rather than on user behavior. This can be an effective way to reach your target audience without relying on cookies.
- **Explore Consent Management Platforms (CMPs):** Consider using a CMP to help you manage user consent and ensure compliance with data privacy regulations.
- **Focus on Creative and Messaging:** Invest in creating compelling ad creatives and messaging that resonate with your target audience, even with limited targeting options.
- **Use Google's Conversion Modeling:** Google is developing conversion modeling to estimate conversions from users who haven't given consent for tracking. This can help you get a more accurate picture of your campaign performance.

Quick Wins for Consent Mode v2:

- **Update Your Privacy Policy:** Make sure your privacy policy is clear, concise, and up-to-date with the latest regulations.
- **Implement a CMP:** Choose a reliable CMP to manage user consent and ensure compliance.

- **Review and Adjust Your Campaigns:** Analyze your paid advertising campaigns and make adjustments to your targeting and bidding strategies as needed to adapt to the changes brought about by Consent Mode v2.
- **Focus on Quality Over Quantity:** Prioritize creating high-quality ads that resonate with your audience, even if you have a smaller reach due to consent restrictions.

By understanding and adapting to Consent Mode v2, you can ensure that your paid advertising campaigns remain effective, compliant, and respectful of user privacy.

Real-World Examples: Paid Advertising Success Stories

- **Local Restaurant Increases Foot Traffic with Google Ads:** A small family-owned restaurant in a competitive market struggled to attract new customers. They created targeted Google Ads campaigns that appeared when people searched for "restaurants near me" or "best Italian food in [city name]." By offering special promotions and highlighting their unique menu items, they were able to drive a significant increase in foot traffic and sales.
- **Online Retailer Boosts Sales with Facebook Retargeting:** An online retailer was experiencing a high rate of cart abandonment. They implemented a Facebook retargeting campaign that showed ads to people who had added items to their cart but didn't complete their purchase. This helped them recover lost sales and increase their overall conversion rate.
- **B2B Company Generates High-Quality Leads with**

LinkedIn Ads: A B2B company wanted to generate leads from decision-makers in their target industry. They created targeted LinkedIn Ads campaigns that showcased their expertise and offered valuable content downloads. This resulted in a steady stream of high-quality leads that converted into paying customers.

These are just a few examples of how paid advertising can be used to achieve a variety of marketing goals. By understanding the different platforms, strategies, and best practices, you can create successful paid advertising campaigns that drive real results for your business.

Common Mistakes to Avoid: Navigating the Paid Advertising Pitfalls

Paid advertising can be a powerful tool, but it's important to avoid common mistakes that can waste your budget and hinder your results. By being aware of these pitfalls, you can steer clear of them and maximize the effectiveness of your campaigns.

- **Poor Targeting:** One of the biggest mistakes businesses make with paid advertising is targeting the wrong audience. Casting a wide net might seem tempting, but it's often more effective to focus on a specific niche. Use the targeting options available on each platform to reach the people most likely to be interested in your products or services.
- **Irrelevant Ad Creatives:** Your ads should be visually appealing and relevant to your target audience. Avoid using generic or stock photos that don't reflect your brand. Instead, use high-quality images or videos that showcase your

products or services in the best possible light. Make sure your visuals align with your brand's aesthetic and resonate with your target audience's interests.
- **Weak Ad Copy:** Your ad copy should be clear, concise, and persuasive. Highlight the unique benefits of your product or service and use a strong call to action. Avoid vague language and generic claims. Instead, focus on specific benefits and use action words that encourage users to click.
- **Neglecting to Track Results:** If you don't track your campaign performance, you won't know what's working and what's not. Use the analytics tools provided by each platform to monitor your results. Track key metrics like impressions, clicks, CTR, conversions, and ROI. This data will help you identify areas for improvement and optimize your campaigns over time.
- **Not Optimizing Your Campaigns:** Paid advertising requires ongoing optimization. Regularly review your campaign performance and make adjustments as needed. Test different ad variations, targeting options, and bidding strategies to see what works best. Don't be afraid to experiment and try new things.

Real-World Examples: Paid Advertising Success Stories

To illustrate the power of paid advertising, let's look at a few examples of small businesses that have achieved significant results:

1. **Local Restaurant Increases Foot Traffic with Google Ads:** A family-owned Italian restaurant in Bucharest was struggling to compete with larger chains in the area. They

decided to run a Google Ads campaign targeting keywords like "best pizza in Bucharest" and "Italian restaurant near me." The campaign was a success, driving a significant increase in website traffic, phone inquiries, and foot traffic.
2. **Handmade Jewelry Business Boosts Sales with Instagram Ads:** A small jewelry maker wanted to increase brand awareness and sales for her online store. She created a series of visually stunning Instagram ads showcasing her unique designs and offering a special discount code for first-time buyers. The campaign generated a surge in website traffic and resulted in a 30% increase in sales within the first month.
3. **B2B Tech Startup Generates Leads with LinkedIn Ads:** A tech startup specializing in software solutions for small businesses wanted to generate high-quality leads. They created targeted LinkedIn ads that spoke directly to the pain points of their ideal customers and offered a free consultation. The campaign generated a steady stream of qualified leads that converted into paying customers at a high rate.

These examples demonstrate the diverse ways in which paid advertising can be used to achieve business goals. By understanding your target audience, crafting compelling ads, and continuously optimizing your campaigns, you can unlock the full potential of paid advertising and drive significant growth for your business.

Putting It All Together: A Paid Advertising Action Plan for Small Businesses

Now that you understand the various paid advertising options, let's create a simplified action plan to help you get started:

1. **Define Your Goals:** Be crystal clear about what you want to achieve with paid advertising. Do you want more website visitors, increased brand visibility, or direct sales? Setting SMART goals will help you measure your success.
2. **Identify Your Target Audience:** Develop detailed buyer personas that represent your ideal customers. Consider their demographics, interests, pain points, and online behavior.
3. **Choose Your Platforms:** Based on your audience and goals, select the platforms that will give you the best reach and engagement. Remember, you don't need to be on every platform; focus on the ones where your customers are most active.
4. **Start with a Small Budget:** Don't overcommit at the beginning. Allocate a small portion of your marketing budget to paid advertising and experiment with different platforms and strategies to see what works best for your business.
5. **Create Compelling Ads:** Craft eye-catching visuals and persuasive ad copy that speaks directly to your target audience's needs and desires.
6. **Track Your Results:** Use analytics tools to monitor your campaign performance and track key metrics like impressions, clicks, CTR, conversions, and ROI. Use this data to make informed decisions and optimize your campaigns for better results.
7. **Be Patient and Persistent:** Paid advertising takes time and effort. Don't expect overnight success. Be patient, persistent, and willing to adapt your strategy as you learn and grow.

Remember:

- Paid advertising is an investment, not an expense.
- Don't be afraid to experiment with different platforms and strategies.
- Track your results and make data-driven decisions to optimize your campaigns.
- Seek professional help if you need guidance or support.

Conclusion

Paid advertising is a powerful tool that can help your small business achieve remarkable growth. By understanding the different platforms and strategies available, crafting compelling ads, and continuously optimizing your campaigns, you can reach a wider audience, drive traffic to your website, and generate leads and sales.

Remember, the key to success with paid advertising is to start small, experiment, track your results, and be patient. With dedication and the right approach, paid advertising can become a valuable asset in your digital marketing arsenal.

7

Refine and Conquer: Your Data-Driven Playbook for Digital Marketing Success

Digital marketing is a dynamic landscape, and success depends on your ability to adapt and evolve. This chapter will empower you to harness the power of data—your most valuable asset—to measure, analyze, and optimize your marketing efforts for continuous growth.

From Vanity Metrics to Actionable Insights

In the world of digital marketing, it's easy to get distracted by so-called "vanity metrics" – those feel-good numbers like likes, shares, and followers. While these metrics may seem impressive, they don't always translate to meaningful business results.

To truly understand the effectiveness of your marketing, focus instead on *actionable insights.* These are the metrics that directly impact your bottom line and reveal how your audience is engaging with your brand.

Channel
  Key Metrics
  Why They Matter

- **Website**
  Traffic, Bounce Rate, Time on Page, Conversion Rate
  Reveal how users interact with your site, which content resonates, and how effective your calls to action are.
  - **Social Media**
  Reach, Impressions, Engagement, Clicks, Conversions
  Measure brand visibility, audience interaction, and the effectiveness of social campaigns in driving action.
  - **Email**
  Open Rate, Click-Through Rate (CTR), Conversions
  Assess email campaign performance, recipient engagement, and how effectively emails are driving desired actions.
  - **Paid Ads**
  Impressions, Clicks, CTR, Cost per Click (CPC), Conversions, Return on Ad Spend (ROAS)
  Evaluate ad performance, cost-effectiveness, and the overall return on your paid advertising investments.

Setting the Stage for Success: Establishing Your Baseline

Before you can analyze and improve, you need a starting point. That's where establishing a baseline comes in.

Steps to Establish Your Baseline:

1. **Set up Analytics:** If you haven't already, install website analytics (e.g., Google Analytics) and utilize the built-in analytics tools provided by social media platforms and email marketing providers.
2. **Choose Key Metrics:** Select the metrics most relevant to your business goals. For instance, if your primary goal is lead generation, focus on tracking website form submissions and email signups.
3. **Benchmark:** Compare your initial data to industry averages or competitor data to gauge your starting position. This context will be crucial as you monitor changes over time.

Pro Tip: Use dashboards or reports to visualize your data for easy analysis. Many tools offer customizable dashboards, or you can create your own using spreadsheets.

Making Data-Driven Decisions: From Insights to Action

Armed with data, you can make informed decisions to optimize your strategies. Here are some examples:

- **Scenario 1: High Website Traffic, Low Conversions:** This suggests that people are finding your website but aren't

taking action. Analyze your website's design, calls to action, and content to identify areas for improvement. You might also consider using A/B testing to compare different versions of your website and see which one performs better.
- **Scenario 2: Low Social Media Engagement:** If your posts aren't generating likes, comments, or shares, experiment with different types of content, posting times, or social media platforms. Look at what your competitors are doing and see if you can glean any insights.
- **Scenario 3: High Email Open Rates, Low CTR:** If people are opening your emails but not clicking on your links, it may be time to revisit your email content or calls to action. Ensure your emails are visually appealing, concise, and relevant to your subscribers' interests.

Quick Tip: Don't be afraid to experiment! Data can help you identify what works and what doesn't, so feel free to try new approaches and see how they impact your results.

Building a Data-Driven Culture

Cultivate a data-driven culture within your organization by:

- **Empowering Your Team:** Encourage your team to utilize data in their decision-making processes.
- **Regular Reporting:** Share key metrics and insights with your team regularly to keep everyone aligned with your goals.
- **Continuous Learning:** Invest in training and resources to help your team improve their data analysis skills.

Real-World Example:

Acme Marketing Solutions, a small agency, transformed their client results by emphasizing data. Each week, they reviewed key metrics, discussed insights, and brainstormed improvements together, leading to more effective campaigns and happier clients.

With a data-driven approach, you can continuously refine your strategies, allocate your budget more effectively, and ultimately achieve greater success in your digital marketing endeavors.

Case Study: Data-Driven Decisions Transform a Local Bookstore

The Book Nook, a cozy independent bookstore in Bucharest, was struggling to compete with online retailers and e-books. They had a loyal following of customers who loved their personalized recommendations and curated selection of books, but their online sales were lagging.

The owner, Maria, decided to take a data-driven approach to her digital marketing. She started by setting up Google Analytics to track website traffic, bounce rates, and conversions. She also implemented social media analytics tools to monitor engagement and reach.

Maria quickly discovered that her website was attracting a decent amount of traffic, but the bounce rate was high, indicating that visitors weren't staying long or taking action. By analyzing user behavior data, she noticed that most visitors were leaving from the homepage, which was cluttered and difficult to navigate.

Armed with this insight, Maria redesigned her homepage,

making it more visually appealing, simplifying the navigation, and adding clear calls to action. She also started tracking which books were most popular on her website and used this data to create targeted email campaigns and social media posts promoting those titles.

Within a few months, Maria saw a significant improvement in her website's performance. The bounce rate decreased, the average time on page increased, and online sales began to climb. By making data-driven decisions, Maria was able to optimize her website and marketing efforts, resulting in increased visibility, engagement, and ultimately, a boost in revenue for her bookstore.

Taking Action: Your Data-Driven Playbook

Remember, data is not just numbers on a screen. It's a treasure trove of insights that can unlock the full potential of your digital marketing efforts. Here's your playbook for data-driven success:

1. **Set Clear Goals:** Define specific, measurable, achievable, relevant, and time-bound (SMART) goals for your digital marketing campaigns.
2. **Track Your Metrics:** Choose the most relevant metrics to track based on your goals and channels.
3. **Analyze Your Data:** Use analytics tools to identify trends, patterns, and areas for improvement.
4. **Experiment and Optimize:** Don't be afraid to try new things and test different strategies. Use A/B testing to compare different versions of your website, ads, or emails.
5. **Make Data-Driven Decisions:** Use your data to inform

your marketing decisions and continuously optimize your campaigns.
6. **Build a Data-Driven Culture:** Empower your team to use data and encourage a culture of experimentation and learning.

Conclusion

By embracing a data-driven approach to digital marketing, you can transform your business. Data allows you to make informed decisions, optimize your strategies, and achieve measurable results. Don't be afraid to experiment, learn from your mistakes, and continuously refine your approach. Remember, data is your compass, guiding you towards success in the ever-evolving digital landscape.

8

Investing in Your Digital Future: A Smart Budgeting Guide for Business Growth

"Marketing is no longer about the stuff that you make, but about the stories you tell."
– Seth Godin

This quote by marketing guru Seth Godin perfectly captures the essence of digital marketing. It's about connecting with your audience, building relationships, and sharing your brand's story in a way that resonates and inspires. But how do you achieve this without breaking the bank?

In this chapter, we'll debunk the myth that digital marketing is only for businesses with deep pockets. You'll discover how to create a smart, strategic, and cost-effective marketing budget that will deliver real results.

From Budgeting to Investing: Fueling Your Growth Engine

Let's reframe the conversation. Instead of thinking about "budgeting" for digital marketing, think of it as "investing" in your business's future. Every dollar you spend on marketing is an investment in building brand awareness, attracting new customers, and ultimately, driving revenue growth.

While digital marketing can seem overwhelming at first, it doesn't have to be expensive or complicated. In fact, many effective strategies can be implemented with little to no cost. And by tracking your results and making data-driven decisions, you can ensure that every dolar you invest in marketing is working hard for your business.

Understanding Your Digital Marketing Investment: What to Expect

Digital marketing encompasses a wide range of channels and strategies, each with its own associated costs. Let's break down the potential investment areas to help you plan your budget:

- **Website Development and Maintenance:** This includes costs for domain registration (around $10-$15 per year), hosting (approximately $5-$50+ per month), website design (which can range from $500 to $5,000+ depending on complexity), development, and ongoing maintenance (e.g., security updates, content updates).
- **Content Creation:** If you're not creating content yourself, you'll need to factor in costs for writers (approximately $50-$200+ per article or blog post), designers, photographers, videographers, or other content creators.
- **SEO:** SEO can be done in-house or outsourced to an agency. Costs may include keyword research tools (monthly subscriptions around $99-$199+), link building services (variable costs depending on the quality and quantity of links), and technical SEO audits (around $500-$1,500+ per audit).

- **Social Media Marketing:** While organic social media is free, you might consider paid advertising campaigns on platforms like Facebook and Instagram. The costs for social media advertising vary depending on your targeting, goals, and ad formats, but you can expect to spend anywhere from $5 to $50+ per day.
- **Email Marketing:** Email marketing platforms usually charge based on the size of your email list and the features you need. For small businesses, you can find plans starting at $10-$20 per month, while larger lists or more advanced features can cost upwards of $100+ per month.
- **Paid Advertising:** Costs for paid advertising can vary widely depending on the platform, targeting options, and competition. For example, Google Ads allows you to set your own budget and bids, so you can control your spending. However, competitive keywords can be expensive, with some clicks costing upwards of $50 or more.

Setting a Realistic Budget: A Roadmap to Success

When setting your digital marketing budget, it's important to be realistic about your resources and expectations. Here's a step-by-step approach to create a budget that works for your business:

1. **Determine Your Overall Marketing Budget:** How much can you afford to invest in marketing each month or quarter? A good starting point is to allocate 5-10% of your projected revenue to marketing.
2. **Allocate Your Budget:** Divide your budget among different digital marketing channels based on your goals, target

audience, and the costs associated with each channel.
3. **Start Small and Scale Up:** Begin with a smaller investment and test different strategies to see what works best for your business. As you see results and gain confidence, you can gradually increase your spending.
4. **Prioritize High-ROI Channels:** Focus on the channels that are most likely to generate a positive return on investment for your business. This might mean investing more in channels like SEO and email marketing, which tend to have lower costs and higher ROI than paid advertising.
5. **Track Your Spending:** Monitor your ad spending closely and analyze your results to identify which campaigns are most effective. Be prepared to adjust your budget allocation based on performance.

Remember, a successful digital marketing budget is not about spending the most money; it's about spending your money wisely and strategically to achieve the best possible results for your business.

Cost-Effective Strategies for Small Businesses: Doing More with Less

As a small business owner, you might feel limited by your budget. However, that doesn't mean you can't achieve significant results with your digital marketing efforts. Here are some clever and resourceful tactics to make the most of every dollar:

1. **Harness the Power of DIY Content Creation:**

- **Be Your Own Content Creator:** If you have a knack for

writing, photography, or video editing, leverage your skills to create your own content.
- **Free Design Tools:** Platforms like Canva offer user-friendly templates and tools to create professional-looking social media graphics, blog post images, and even simple videos.
- **Stock Images and Videos:** Numerous websites offer free or affordable high-quality images and video footage that you can use to enhance your visual content.

2. Master Organic Social Media Marketing:

- **Optimize Your Profiles:** Complete your profiles on relevant platforms with engaging bios, high-quality images, and links to your website.
- **Create Engaging Content:** Share a mix of informative, entertaining, and visually appealing content that aligns with your brand voice.
- **Engage with Your Audience:** Respond to comments, ask questions, and participate in conversations to build a loyal following.
- **Leverage Hashtags:** Research and use relevant hashtags to increase the visibility of your posts.

3. Utilize Email Marketing's Direct Line to Customers:

- **Start with a Free Plan:** Many email marketing platforms offer free plans with limited features for small businesses. Take advantage of these plans to get started with email marketing without incurring costs.
- **Grow Your List Organically:** Offer incentives like discounts or exclusive content in exchange for email addresses. Pro-

mote your email list on your website and social media channels.
- **Personalize Your Messages:** Segment your list and send targeted emails that resonate with each group of subscribers.
- **Automate Email Sequences:** Set up automated email sequences like welcome emails, abandoned cart reminders, and re-engagement campaigns to nurture leads and drive conversions.

4. **Collaborate with Micro-Influencers:**

- **Partner with Niche Influencers:** Look for micro-influencers who have a smaller but highly engaged following in your target market.
- **Offer Product or Service Exchanges:** Instead of paying influencers with cash, offer them free products or services in exchange for promotion.
- **Build Authentic Relationships:** Focus on building genuine relationships with influencers who align with your brand values and whose audience matches your target market.

5. **Engage in Online Communities:**

- **Participate in Relevant Forums and Groups:** Share your expertise, answer questions, and build relationships with potential customers in online communities related to your industry.
- **Be Helpful and Authentic:** Don't just promote your business; focus on providing value and building genuine connections.
- **Share Your Content:** Promote your blog posts, articles, or

videos in relevant groups or forums where appropriate.

6. Repurpose and Maximize Your Content:

- **One Piece, Multiple Formats:** Turn a single piece of content into various formats. For example, a blog post can be transformed into a video, an infographic, or several social media posts.
- **Evergreen Content:** Create content that remains relevant and valuable over time. This allows you to continue promoting it and driving traffic to your website.

7. Leverage User-Generated Content:

- **Encourage Customers to Share:** Run contests, offer incentives, or simply ask your customers to share photos or videos of themselves using your products or services.
- **Feature UGC on Your Channels:** Share user-generated content on your website and social media channels to build social proof and trust.

Budgeting Tips: Making Every Dollar Count

Here are a few more specific tips for creating and managing a digital marketing budget that delivers results:

- **Track Everything:** Monitor your spending on every marketing channel and campaign. Use spreadsheets or budgeting software to keep track of your expenses.
- **Analyze Your ROI:** Calculate the return on investment for each campaign to determine which ones are most effective.

This will help you make informed decisions about where to allocate your resources in the future.
- **Don't Be Afraid to Adjust:** Your budget should be flexible. If a particular campaign is not performing well, don't be afraid to reallocate your resources to a more effective channel.
- **Get Creative:** Look for free or low-cost alternatives to expensive marketing tools and services.
- **Partner with Other Businesses:** Collaborate with other businesses in your industry to share marketing costs and cross-promote each other's products or services.

Measuring ROI: The Key to Paid Advertising Success

Measuring the return on investment (ROI) of your paid advertising campaigns is essential for understanding their effectiveness and making informed decisions about your marketing strategy. One of the most important metrics for paid advertising is Return on Ad Spend (ROAS).

Understanding ROAS

ROAS stands for Return on Ad Spend. It measures the revenue generated for every dollar you spend on advertising. In other words, it tells you how much you earn for every dollar you invest in ads.

- **High ROAS:** A high ROAS indicates that your ads are effective and generating a good return on your investment.
- **Low ROAS:** A low ROAS suggests that your ads may not be performing well and that you might need to adjust your strategy.

Calculating ROAS

The formula for calculating ROAS is simple:
ROAS = (Revenue Generated from Ads / Ad Spend) x 100
Example:
If you spent $500 on Facebook Ads and generated $2,000 in revenue from those ads, your ROAS would be 400% (($2,000 / $500) x 100). This means that for every dollar you spent on Facebook Ads, you earned $4 in revenue.

Why ROAS Matters
ROAS is a valuable metric because it allows you to:

- **Evaluate Campaign Performance:** Determine which campaigns are most effective at generating revenue.
- **Optimize Your Budget:** Identify areas where you can allocate your budget more effectively to maximize your ROI.
- **Make Data-Driven Decisions:** Base your advertising decisions on concrete data rather than guesswork.

Important Considerations:

- **ROAS is Not the Only Metric:** While ROAS is important, it's not the only metric you should consider. Other metrics like click-through rate (CTR), conversion rate, and cost per acquisition (CPA) can also provide valuable insights into your campaign performance.
- **ROAS Can Vary:** Your ROAS can vary depending on a variety of factors, such as your industry, target audience, ad platform, and campaign goals. It's important to benchmark your ROAS against industry averages and your own historical data to get a better understanding of what constitutes a "good" ROAS for your business.
- **Long-Term vs. Short-Term:** Some campaigns may have a

lower ROAS in the short term but generate higher lifetime value from customers in the long run. Consider both short-term and long-term goals when evaluating your ROAS.

By understanding ROAS and tracking it alongside other key metrics, you can make informed decisions about your paid advertising strategy and ensure that your campaigns are delivering the best possible results for your business.

9

Building a Strong Brand Presence: Crafting a Story That Sells

In the vast digital landscape, a strong brand presence is more than just a recognizable logo or catchy tagline. It's the essence of your business—the unique story, personality, and values that set you apart from the competition and resonate with your audience. This chapter will guide you through the process of defining your brand, crafting a compelling brand story, creating a consistent brand experience, and managing your online reputation.

Defining Your Brand: More Than Just a Logo

Your brand is more than just a logo, a color scheme, or a catchy slogan. It's the sum total of your customers' perceptions and experiences with your business. It's how they feel about your products or services, the values they associate with your company, and the emotions you evoke in them.

Think of your brand as a person. It has a personality, a voice, a story to tell. And just like a person, your brand needs to be authentic, relatable, and memorable to stand out from the crowd.

Key Elements of Your Brand:

- **Brand Purpose:** What is the driving force behind your business? What problem are you solving, or what need are you fulfilling? Your brand purpose is the reason you exist.
- **Brand Values:** What principles guide your business decisions and actions? What do you stand for? Your brand values are the core beliefs that shape your brand's identity.
- **Brand Personality:** What kind of personality do you want your brand to have? Is it friendly and approachable, sophisticated and elegant, or bold and innovative? Your brand personality should align with your target audience and the image you want to project.
- **Brand Voice:** How do you communicate with your audience? What kind of language, tone, and style do you use? Your brand voice should be consistent across all your marketing channels, both online and offline.
- **Visual Identity:** Your visual identity includes your logo, color palette, typography, and other visual elements. These elements should be visually appealing, memorable, and consistent with your brand personality and values.

Exercise: Define Your Brand

Take a moment to reflect on the following questions:

1. What is the purpose of my business?
2. What are the core values that guide my decisions and actions?
3. What kind of personality do I want my brand to have?

4. How do I want to communicate with my audience?
5. What visual elements best represent my brand?

By answering these questions, you'll gain a deeper understanding of your brand and its unique identity. This will serve as a foundation for all your marketing efforts and help you create a consistent and compelling brand experience for your customers.

Brand Storytelling: The Heart of Your Brand

Stories are powerful tools for connecting with people. They have the ability to evoke emotions, create memories, and inspire action. By crafting a compelling brand story, you can tap into these powerful forces and forge a deeper connection with your audience.

Your brand story is the narrative that explains who you are, what you do, and why you do it. It should be authentic, relatable, and memorable. It should highlight your unique value proposition and explain how your products or services can solve your customers' problems or fulfill their needs.

Elements of a Compelling Brand Story:

- **Authenticity:** Your story should be genuine and reflect the true essence of your brand.
- **Relatability:** Your story should resonate with your target audience and make them feel a connection to your brand.
- **Emotion:** Your story should evoke emotions in your audience, whether it's joy, inspiration, or a sense of shared struggle.
- **Conflict and Resolution:** Your story should have a clear conflict or challenge that is overcome, demonstrating the

value and impact of your brand.

Quick Tip:
Don't be afraid to inject personality and humor into your brand story. People are more likely to remember a story that makes them laugh or feel a strong emotion.

Creating a Consistent Brand Experience: Leaving a Lasting Impression

Consistency is key when it comes to building a strong brand presence. Ensure that your brand elements are used consistently across all your online and offline channels. This includes your website, social media profiles, email marketing, advertising, packaging, and even your customer service interactions.

A consistent brand experience helps to reinforce your brand message and create a cohesive image in the minds of your customers. It also makes your brand more recognizable and memorable, increasing brand recall and loyalty.

Tips for Creating a Consistent Brand Experience:

- **Develop a Brand Style Guide:** A brand style guide outlines the specific rules and guidelines for using your brand elements, including logo usage, color palette, typography, and voice and tone.
- **Train Your Team:** Ensure that everyone in your organization understands your brand identity and values, and that they communicate consistently with customers and the public.
- **Monitor Your Online Presence:** Regularly review your website, social media profiles, and other online channels to

ensure that your brand is being represented accurately and consistently.

Real-World Example:

Consider the brand experience of *Nike*. From their iconic "Just Do It" slogan to their powerful athlete endorsements, every touchpoint with Nike reinforces their brand message of empowerment, athleticism, and perseverance. This consistent brand experience has helped Nike become one of the most recognizable and successful brands in the world.

Online Reputation Management: Safeguarding Your Brand Image

In the digital age, your online reputation can make or break your business. A single negative review or social media comment can quickly spread and damage your brand's image. That's why it's crucial to actively manage your online reputation and address any negative feedback promptly and professionally.

Tips for Online Reputation Management:

- **Monitor Your Online Presence:** Use social listening tools to track mentions of your brand on social media and review sites. Set up Google Alerts to receive notifications whenever your brand is mentioned online.
- **Respond to Reviews and Feedback:** Whether it's positive or negative, respond to all reviews and feedback promptly and professionally. Thank customers for positive feedback and address any concerns raised in negative reviews.
- **Encourage Positive Reviews:** Ask satisfied customers to leave reviews on platforms like Google My Business, Yelp,

or Facebook.
- **Address Negative Feedback Proactively:** If you receive negative feedback, don't ignore it or get defensive. Respond calmly and professionally, and offer solutions to address the customer's concerns.
- **Create Positive Content:** Publish positive content about your brand, such as blog posts, articles, or social media posts highlighting your achievements, customer success stories, or community involvement. This can help to counter any negative information that may be circulating online.

By actively managing your online reputation, you can protect your brand's image, build trust with your audience, and create a positive online presence that will attract and retain customers.

Conclusion

Your brand is more than just a name or a logo; it's the emotional connection you forge with your customers, the values you embody, and the promise you deliver. Building a strong brand presence is an ongoing journey that requires thoughtful planning, consistent execution, and unwavering dedication. But the rewards are worth it.

A strong brand:

- **Attracts and Retains Customers:** People are more likely to buy from brands they know, like, and trust.
- **Commands Premium Prices:** Strong brands can charge more for their products or services because customers perceive them as being of higher quality and value.

- **Creates Brand Advocates:** Loyal customers who love your brand will spread the word and become your most powerful marketing asset.
- **Protects Your Reputation:** A strong brand reputation can help you weather storms and emerge from crises stronger than ever.
- **Drives Long-Term Growth:** A strong brand is a sustainable competitive advantage that can fuel your business growth for years to come.

By defining your brand, crafting a compelling story, creating a consistent brand experience, and actively managing your online reputation, you can build a brand that stands the test of time and propels your business to new heights.

Real-World Example: Local Romanian Artisan Brand Creates a Global Following

Maramureș Weavers, a small weaving cooperative in the heart of Romania, was struggling to sell their beautifully handcrafted textiles in a global market dominated by mass-produced goods. By embracing their unique heritage and cultural traditions, they were able to build a strong brand story that resonated with conscious consumers around the world. They showcased their artisans, their sustainable practices, and the rich history behind their weaving techniques.

Through a combination of social media storytelling, influencer collaborations, and a stunningly designed website, they were able to reach a global audience and create a thriving online business. Their authentic brand story and commitment to quality craftsmanship resonated with customers who were seeking unique, handcrafted products with a meaningful story.

Maramureș Weavers is a shining example of how a small business can leverage brand building to overcome challenges, reach new markets, and achieve remarkable success.

Your Next Steps: Building Your Brand

Remember, building a brand is an ongoing journey. It requires constant attention and dedication. But by following the principles outlined in this chapter and investing in your brand, you can create a loyal following of customers who will support your business for years to come.

Here are a few actionable steps you can take right now:

1. **Start with Your "Why":** Clarify your brand purpose and values. What are you passionate about? What impact do you want to make in the world?
2. **Tell Your Story:** Craft a compelling brand story that connects with your audience on an emotional level.
3. **Create a Visual Identity:** Develop a logo, color palette, and typography that reflect your brand's personality and values.
4. **Be Consistent:** Ensure that your brand message and visuals are consistent across all your marketing channels.
5. **Monitor Your Reputation:** Actively manage your online reputation and address any negative feedback promptly and professionally.

By taking these steps, you'll be well on your way to building a strong brand presence that will attract and retain customers, differentiate you from the competition, and propel your business to new heights of success.

10

Local SEO: Dominating Your Local Market

As a small business owner, you know that competition can be fierce. But did you know that a significant portion of your potential customers are searching online for businesses *just like yours*? That's where local SEO comes in. It's your secret weapon for attracting those nearby customers who are ready to spend. In this chapter, we'll break down the specific strategies and tactics that will help your business rise to the top of local search results and become the go-to choice for customers in your area.

Understanding Local SEO: What Makes It Different

Local SEO is a specialized branch of SEO that focuses on optimizing your online presence to attract more business from relevant local searches. It differs from traditional SEO in several ways:

- **Focus on Local Keywords:** While traditional SEO targets broader keywords, local SEO prioritizes keywords that include your location (e.g., "[your service/product] in [your

city]," "best [your product/service] near me").
- **Google My Business Optimization:** Your Google My Business (GMB) listing is a critical component of local SEO. It's the information panel that appears when someone searches for your business on Google. Optimizing your GMB listing is essential for appearing in the "local pack" (the top three local results) and Google Maps.
- **Local Citations:** Local citations are online mentions of your business name, address, and phone number (NAP). These citations help search engines verify your business's legitimacy and location.
- **Online Reviews:** Positive reviews on platforms like Google, Yelp, and Facebook can significantly impact your local search rankings and influence potential customers' decisions.

Why Local SEO Matters: Reaching Your Neighbors

For businesses that rely on local customers, local SEO can be a game-changer. Here's why:

- **Increased Visibility in Local Search Results:** When potential customers search for businesses like yours in your area, you want your business to be at the top of the results. Local SEO helps you achieve this by optimizing your website and online presence for local keywords and phrases.
- **More Foot Traffic and Phone Calls:** By appearing in the local pack and Google Maps, you're more likely to attract people actively seeking businesses nearby. This can translate to increased visits to your physical location and a boost in phone inquiries.

- **Higher Conversion Rates:** People who find your business through local search are often ready to buy. They're already in your area and looking for a solution to their problem, making them more likely to become paying customers.
- **Enhanced Brand Reputation:** A strong local SEO presence builds your brand's credibility within the community. Positive reviews and consistent information across platforms demonstrate your professionalism and commitment to serving the local market.

Local SEO Strategies: Your Roadmap to Local Dominance

Here's your roadmap to conquering your local market with local SEO:

1. **Google My Business (GMB) Optimization:**

- **Claim and Verify:** If you haven't already, claim your GMB listing and ensure all details are accurate and up-to-date.
- **NAP Consistency:** Double-check that your name, address, and phone number (NAP) match your website and other online listings.
- **Categories:** Choose the most relevant categories for your business.
- **Photos and Videos:** Upload high-quality visuals that showcase your business and products.
- **Posts:** Share regular updates, promotions, and events.
- **Q&A:** Monitor and respond to customer questions on your GMB listing.
- **GMB Insights:** Utilize GMB's analytics to track your performance and identify areas for improvement.

1. **Build Local Citations:**

- **List Your Business:** Ensure your business is listed on major directories like Google My Business, Facebook, Yelp, Bing Places, and Foursquare.
- **Industry-Specific Directories:** Seek out and list your business in relevant directories specific to your industry (e.g., restaurant guides for a restaurant, legal directories for a law firm).
- **Local Business Associations:** Join local business associations and chambers of commerce to build your local network and earn citations.

1. **Quick Tip:** Use a tool like Moz Local or BrightLocal to check your online citations for accuracy and consistency.
2. **Create Local Content:**

- **Blog Posts:** Write blog posts about local events, news, or topics relevant to your community.
- **Social Media:** Share updates about your business, highlight local customers, and participate in community discussions.
- **Local Partnerships:** Collaborate with other local businesses to cross-promote and create content together.

1. **Optimize for Local Keywords:**

- **Location-Specific Keywords:** Incorporate phrases like "in [your city]," "near [specific neighborhood]," or "serving [your area]" in your website content, title tags, meta descriptions, and header tags.
- **Google Keyword Planner:** Use this free tool to research

relevant local keywords and their search volumes.

1. **Encourage and Manage Online Reviews:**

- **Ask for Reviews:** Proactively ask satisfied customers to leave reviews on Google, Facebook, Yelp, or other relevant platforms.
- **Respond to Reviews:** Address both positive and negative reviews promptly and professionally. Thank customers for their feedback and show that you value their opinions.

Quick Wins for Local SEO:

- **NAP Consistency:** Ensure your business name, address, and phone number are consistent across all online platforms.
- **Mobile Optimization:** Make sure your website is mobile-friendly, as many local searches are conducted on smartphones.
- **Local Link Building:** Get backlinks from other local businesses, organizations, or websites.
- **Optimize for Voice Search:** As voice search becomes more popular, optimize your content for voice queries by using natural language and long-tail keywords.
- **Use Location Pages:** If your business has multiple locations, create dedicated pages for each location on your website.
- **Get Listed in Local Directories:** Ensure your business is listed in relevant local directories like Yelp, Yellow Pages, and industry-specific directories.

Local SEO Case Study: Coffee Shop Brews Success with Local SEO

The Daily Grind, a cozy independent coffee shop in a bustling city, was passionate about their craft coffee and warm ambiance. However, despite their loyal regulars, they were struggling to attract new customers, especially those who weren't familiar with the area.

The Challenge:

The owners of *The Daily Grind* knew that they needed to expand their reach and increase their online visibility to attract a larger audience. They decided to focus their efforts on local SEO to attract more customers searching online for coffee shops in their city.

The Solution:

The Daily Grind partnered with a local SEO expert to develop a comprehensive strategy. This included:

- Optimizing their Google My Business listing with accurate information, photos, and regular posts.
- Building local citations by listing their business on relevant directories.
- Creating a blog with content about the local coffee scene, brewing tips, and their unique offerings.
- Engaging with customers on social media and encouraging them to leave reviews.

The Results:

Within a few months, The Daily Grind saw a significant increase in website traffic, foot traffic, and sales. Their Google My Business listing consistently ranked among the top results for relevant searches, and they became a popular destination for coffee lovers in the area. The increase in visibility led to a substantial boost in sales, allowing them to expand their menu and hire additional staff.

Conclusion

Local SEO is a powerful tool that can help your small business thrive in the digital age. By optimizing your online presence for local search, you can attract more customers, build brand awareness, and establish yourself as a leader in your community. While it may seem daunting at first, the strategies outlined in this chapter are easy to implement and can yield significant results.

Remember, local SEO is an ongoing process, not a one-time fix. By consistently optimizing your website, building citations, creating local content, and engaging with your audience, you can ensure that your business remains at the top of local search results and continues to attract new customers.

With the right approach and a little effort, you can dominate your local market and achieve long-term success.

11

Future-Proof Your Marketing: Embracing Innovation for Lasting Growth

In the fast-paced world of digital marketing, staying ahead of the curve is essential for sustained growth. This chapter will equip you with insights into the cutting-edge trends and technologies that are transforming the industry, and guide you on how to leverage them to stay competitive and future-proof your business.

Artificial Intelligence (AI) in Marketing: Beyond the Buzzword

AI is more than just a buzzword; it's a game-changer that's revolutionizing the way businesses interact with their customers and optimize their marketing campaigns. From chatbots to predictive analytics, AI tools offer new possibilities to enhance customer experiences, streamline operations, and drive growth.

How AI is Transforming Marketing:

- **Hyper-Personalization:** AI analyzes vast amounts of customer data to deliver tailored messages, offers, and recommendations, boosting engagement and conversions. For instance, an online clothing store can use AI to recommend products based on a customer's past purchases and browsing behavior.
- **Predictive Analytics:** By identifying patterns in customer behavior, AI can predict future actions and trends, allowing you to proactively adjust your marketing strategies. This can be particularly useful for anticipating customer churn or identifying potential sales opportunities.
- **Chatbots and Virtual Assistants:** These AI-powered tools provide instant customer support, answer questions, and guide users through the sales funnel, improving customer satisfaction and freeing up your team's time. Many Romanian businesses are already using chatbots on their websites and social media pages to improve customer service and engagement.
- **Content Generation:** AI-powered tools can help you create data-driven content that resonates with your audience, from blog posts to social media captions. Some AI tools can even generate entire articles or product descriptions, saving you time and resources.
- **Ad Optimization:** AI can analyze ad performance data and automatically adjust bids and targeting to improve your campaigns' effectiveness. This means you can get more out of your advertising budget and achieve better results.

Integrating AI into Your Marketing Strategy (with Real-World Examples):

- **Chatbots:** Many Romanian businesses, like eMAG, a leading online retailer, use chatbots to provide 24/7 customer support and answer frequently asked questions. This improves customer satisfaction and frees up their customer service team to focus on more complex issues.
- **Personalized Product Recommendations:** Fashion Days, a popular online fashion retailer in Romania, uses AI-powered algorithms to offer personalized product recommendations to their customers, increasing engagement and boosting sales.
- **Social Media Content Generation:** Several social media management tools like Lately or Phrasee use AI to help businesses create engaging and effective social media posts.

Quick Wins with AI:

- **Start with Simple Tools:** You don't need to invest in expensive AI platforms. Many affordable or even free AI-powered tools are available for small businesses, such as chatbots, social media content generators, and email marketing automation tools.
- **Focus on High-Impact Areas:** Identify the areas where AI can have the most significant impact on your business and start there. For example, if customer service is a major pain point, consider implementing an AI chatbot.
- **Experiment and Learn:** Don't be afraid to try different AI tools and see what works best for your business. The AI landscape is constantly evolving, so stay up-to-date with the latest developments and be willing to adapt your strategies.

Beyond Text: The Rise of Visual and Interactive Content

While written content remains essential, visual and interactive content are becoming increasingly important in capturing your audience's attention and driving engagement.

- **Video Marketing:** From short-form videos on TikTok to live streams on social media, video is a powerful tool for storytelling, showcasing products, and building brand awareness. Consider creating product demos, behind-the-scenes glimpses of your business, customer testimonials, or educational videos related to your industry.
- **Interactive Content:** Quizzes, polls, calculators, and augmented reality (AR) experiences can captivate your audience and encourage them to interact with your brand. For example, a furniture store could create an AR app that allows customers to visualize how furniture would look in their homes.
- **User-Generated Content (UGC):** Encourage your customers to create and share content related to your brand. This could be reviews, testimonials, photos, or videos. UGC is authentic, engaging, and can build trust with potential customers. Consider running contests or offering incentives to encourage customers to share their experiences with your brand.

Tips for Creating Engaging Visual and Interactive Content:

- **Tell a Story:** Use visuals to tell a compelling story that resonates with your audience. Craft a narrative that highlights your brand's unique value proposition and connects with

your customers' emotions.
- **Focus on Quality:** Invest in high-quality visuals and ensure your content is visually appealing and easy to consume. Use professional-grade cameras, microphones, and editing software if possible.
- **Keep it Interactive:** Encourage participation and interaction by asking questions, running contests, or creating interactive experiences. For example, you could create a quiz related to your industry or offer a virtual tour of your business.

Example: A local restaurant in Bucharest could partner with a food blogger to create a video showcasing their signature dishes. The video could include behind-the-scenes footage of the chefs preparing the food, interviews with customers, and mouthwatering shots of the finished dishes.

Beyond Google: Diversifying Your Traffic Sources

While Google remains the dominant search engine, it's important to diversify your traffic sources to reduce reliance on a single platform. Here are a few alternative channels to consider:

- **Social Media:** Drive traffic to your website by sharing your content and engaging with your audience on social media platforms.
- **Email Marketing:** Build an email list and send regular newsletters with valuable content and promotions to nurture leads and drive sales.
- **Referral Traffic:** Partner with other businesses, influencers, or websites to exchange backlinks and drive referral traffic

to your site.
- **Paid Advertising:** Invest in paid advertising campaigns on platforms like Facebook, Instagram, LinkedIn, or Pinterest to reach a wider audience and target specific demographics.

The Future of Data Privacy and Security

As consumers become more aware of their online privacy, businesses must prioritize data protection and transparency.

Key considerations for data privacy and security:

- **Transparency:** Be transparent about how you collect, use, and share customer data. Clearly communicate your privacy policy and give users control over their data.
- **Consent:** Obtain explicit consent from users before collecting their data. Use clear and concise language in your consent forms, and avoid pre-checked boxes or other deceptive practices.
- **Data Security:** Implement robust security measures to protect customer data from unauthorized access or breaches. This includes using strong passwords, encrypting sensitive data, and regularly backing up your data.
- **Compliance:** Stay up-to-date with relevant data protection regulations like GDPR in Europe and CCPA in California.

Conclusion

The digital marketing landscape is constantly evolving, and staying ahead of the curve is crucial for long-term success. By embracing emerging trends like AI, voice search, and video marketing, diversifying your traffic sources, and prioritizing data privacy and security, you can future-proof your business and ensure that your marketing efforts remain effective and relevant.

Remember, the key is to stay informed, adapt to change, and always prioritize providing value to your customers. With the right strategies and a willingness to embrace innovation, you can navigate the future of digital marketing with confidence and achieve lasting growth for your business.

12

Your Digital Marketing Toolkit: Resources for Success

You now have a solid foundation in the core concepts and strategies of digital marketing. This chapter serves as your toolkit, equipping you with additional resources to refine your skills, find the right tools, and continue your journey toward digital marketing mastery.

Glossary of Digital Marketing Terms

Digital marketing is full of specialized terminology. This glossary will help you navigate the jargon and understand the key terms and concepts you'll encounter as you delve deeper into the world of online marketing.

- **A/B Testing:** A method of comparing two versions of a webpage, ad, or email to see which one performs better.
- **Algorithm:** A set of rules or instructions that a computer program follows to solve a problem or complete a task. Search engines use algorithms to rank websites in search

results.
- **Analytics:** The collection, measurement, and analysis of website data to understand user behavior and optimize website performance.
- **Backlink:** A link from one website to another. Backlinks are important for SEO because they signal to search engines that your website is trustworthy and authoritative.
- **Bounce Rate:** The percentage of visitors who leave your website after viewing only one page.
- **Buyer Persona:** A semi-fictional representation of your ideal customer based on market research and real data about your existing customers.
- **Call to Action (CTA):** A phrase or button that encourages users to take a specific action, such as "Shop Now," "Learn More," or "Sign Up."
- **Click-Through Rate (CTR):** The percentage of people who click on a link in an email or advertisement.
- **Content Marketing:** A strategic marketing approach focused on creating and distributing valuable, relevant, and consistent content to attract and retain a clearly defined audience.
- **Conversion Rate:** The percentage of website visitors who complete a desired action, such as making a purchase, filling out a form, or subscribing to a newsletter.
- **Cost Per Acquisition (CPA):** The average amount of money you spend to acquire a new customer or lead.
- **Customer Journey:** The complete sum of experiences that customers go through when interacting with your company and brand.
- **Email Marketing:** The use of email to promote products or services, build relationships with customers, and drive

sales.
- **Google Ads:** Google's advertising platform, which allows businesses to display ads on Google search results pages and other websites.
- **Google Analytics:** A free web analytics service offered by Google that tracks and reports website traffic.
- **Impressions:** The number of times an advertisement is displayed, whether it is clicked or not.
- **Influencer Marketing:** A form of marketing that involves collaborating with influencers (people with a large and engaged following) to promote your brand or products.
- **Keyword:** A word or phrase that people use to search for information online.
- **Landing Page:** The webpage that a user is directed to after clicking on an advertisement or link.
- **Lead:** A potential customer who has expressed interest in your product or service.
- **Organic Search:** Search engine results that are not paid advertisements.
- **Paid Advertising:** Advertising that involves paying to display your ads on various platforms, such as search engines, social media, and websites.
- **Pay-Per-Click (PPC):** An advertising model where advertisers pay a fee each time one of their ads is clicked.
- **Remarketing/Retargeting:** A form of online advertising that allows you to target ads to people who have previously visited your website or interacted with your brand.
- **Return on Investment (ROI):** A measure of the profitability of an investment, calculated as the net profit divided by the cost of the investment.
- **Search Engine Optimization (SEO):** The process of opti-

mizing your website and content to rank higher in search engine results pages (SERPs).
- **Social Media Marketing:** The use of social media platforms to connect with your audience, build brand awareness, and drive website traffic.

Templates and Checklists

To make implementing your digital marketing strategies easier, we've included a few helpful templates and checklists:

- **Content Calendar Template:** Plan and schedule your content across various channels with this handy template.

Date
Topic/Title
Content Type
Channel
Author/Owner
Notes

- **Social Media Contest Checklist:** Ensure your social media contests are successful with this comprehensive checklist.

1. Define clear goals.
2. Identify your target audience.
3. Choose a relevant prize.
4. Create clear and concise rules.
5. Promote your contest across all channels.

6. Use eye-catching visuals.
7. Track and analyze results.

- **Google Ads Campaign Setup Checklist:** Launch your Google Ads campaigns with confidence using this step-by-step checklist.

1. Define your campaign goals and target audience.
2. Set a budget and bidding strategy.
3. Conduct keyword research.
4. Create compelling ad copy and visuals.
5. Set up conversion tracking.
6. Monitor and optimize your campaign performance.

Recommended Tools and Resources (Free/Affordable)

Here's a curated list of digital marketing tools and resources that are perfect for small businesses with limited budgets:

- **Website Builders:** Wix, WordPress, Squarespace
- **SEO Tools:** Google Search Console, Ubersuggest, Moz Local
- **Social Media Management Tools:** Buffer, Hootsuite, Later
- **Email Marketing Platforms:** Mailchimp, Sendinblue, MailerLite
- **Graphic Design Tools:** Canva, Crello
- **Video Editing Tools:** InShot, Kapwing, CapCut
- **Analytics Tools:** Google Analytics
- **Social Listening Tools:** Mention, Hootsuite Insights

Recommended Resources

- **Moz Blog:** A comprehensive resource for SEO and digital marketing knowledge.
- **Neil Patel:** A renowned digital marketing expert offering valuable insights on his blog and YouTube channel.
- **Social Media Examiner:** A website packed with social media marketing tips, guides, and case studies.
- **HubSpot Blog:** A hub for inbound marketing, content marketing, and social media marketing resources.
- **Google Digital Garage:** Free online courses on digital marketing fundamentals.

This toolkit provides you with the essential resources to navigate the digital marketing landscape with confidence. Remember, continuous learning and experimentation are key to success.

13

Your Journey to Digital Marketing Mastery

Congratulations! You've now embarked on an exciting journey into the world of digital marketing. Throughout this book, we've explored the essential tools, strategies, and tactics that can empower your business to thrive in the digital age. From building a strong online foundation to attracting your ideal customers, creating compelling content, harnessing the power of paid advertising, and measuring your success, you've gained a comprehensive understanding of the digital marketing landscape.

Key Takeaways:

- **Embrace the Power of Digital:** Digital marketing is not just a trend; it's a necessity for business growth in the modern age. It offers a cost-effective and efficient way to reach your target audience, build brand awareness, and drive sales.
- **Build a Strong Online Foundation:** Your website is your digital storefront and should be a top priority. Invest in a well-designed, user-friendly website that reflects your

brand identity and provides a seamless user experience.
- **Know Your Audience, Inside and Out:** Understanding your ideal customers is crucial for crafting marketing messages that resonate. Develop detailed buyer personas to guide your strategies.
- **Content is King:** Create high-quality, valuable content that educates, entertains, and inspires your audience. Share your expertise, tell your brand story, and showcase your products or services in a way that connects with your customers.
- **Promote Your Content Strategically:** Utilize a variety of channels like social media, email marketing, and paid advertising to amplify your reach and attract more potential customers.
- **Measure, Analyze, Optimize:** Track your marketing performance, analyze your data, and make data-driven decisions to continually improve your campaigns and achieve your goals.
- **Embrace Innovation:** Stay ahead of the curve by embracing emerging trends and technologies like AI, voice search, video marketing, and interactive content.

Your Roadmap to Success:

1. **Define Your Brand:** Clarify your brand purpose, values, personality, and voice.
2. **Craft a Compelling Story:** Share your brand's unique story to connect with your audience on a deeper level.
3. **Optimize Your Website:** Make your website user-friendly, mobile-responsive, and fast.
4. **Master SEO:** Implement SEO best practices to improve your visibility in search results.

5. **Leverage Social Media:** Build a strong presence on social media platforms that resonate with your target audience.
6. **Harness Email Marketing:** Nurture leads and drive sales through targeted email campaigns.
7. **Explore Paid Advertising:** Consider investing in paid advertising to accelerate your growth.
8. **Measure Your Results:** Track key metrics, analyze data, and optimize your campaigns for maximum ROI.
9. **Embrace Innovation:** Stay up-to-date with the latest trends and technologies to future-proof your business.

Remember: Digital marketing is an ongoing journey of learning, experimentation, and adaptation. With dedication, perseverance, and a data-driven approach, you can achieve remarkable success and build a thriving business in the digital age.

The digital world is your oyster. Go forth and conquer!

Your Success is Our Success

We hope this guide has equipped you with the knowledge and confidence to take your digital marketing to new heights. As you implement these strategies and watch your business grow, remember that your success is our success. We're here to cheer you on and celebrate your achievements. Now go out there and make your mark on the digital world!

www.ingramcontent.com/pod-product-compliance
Lightning Source LLC
Chambersburg PA
CBHW071930210526
45479CB00002B/627